Brain Boosters for Business Advantage

Ticklers, Grab Bags, Blue Skies, and Other Bionic Ideas

BRAIN BOOSTERS FOR BUSINESS ADVANTAGE

TICKLERS, GRAB BAGS, BLUE SKIES, AND OTHER BIONIC IDEAS

Arthur B. VanGundy

Pfeiffer
& COMPANY

Amsterdam • Johannesburg • Oxford
San Diego • Sydney • Toronto

Library of Congress Cataloging-in-Publication Data
VanGundy, Arthur B.

Brain boosters for business advantage: ticklers, grab bags, blue skies, and other bionic ideas / Arthur B. VanGundy.

p.   cm.

Includes bibliographical references and index.

ISBN 0-89384-267-2

1. Creative ability in business. 2. Problem solving. 3. Creative thinking.   I. title.

HD53.V358   1994

153.4'3—dc20

94-31011

CIP

Dedication

This book is dedicated to my father,
Arthur B. VanGundy, M.D., and in loving
memory to my mother, Sarajane Miesse
VanGundy, who helped boost my creativity
by their wit, example, and love.

Contents

CHAPTER 6
Combinations   121

CHAPTER 7
Blue Skies   157

PART 3: GROUP BRAIN BOOSTERS   221

Acknowledgments

The boosters in this book are based on the ideas and efforts of many people. German creativity consultant Horst Geschka and his associates devised many of the boosters, especially the brainwriting ones. I am indebted to their pioneering work in this field going back to the early 1970s. Michael Michalko certainly has had an impact on the creativity field with his idea generation methods, and I am grateful to him for his contributions.

I am especially indebted to professional inventor Doug Hall of Richard Saunders International for his creative contributions to the field of idea generation. Doug is a true innovator who has a unique ability to transform and package traditional idea generation methods in almost magical ways. Thank you, Doug, for your friendship and generous sharing of your ideas and techniques.

I would also like to thank all of the students, seminar participants, and consulting clients who have increased my understanding of creativity and idea generation. I have learned a lot from these people over the past eighteen years as a professor and consultant. I look forward to learning more and growing with them over the next eighteen plus years.

Finally, I would like to thank my wife, Donna Nelson, for her support and encouragement during the writing of this book.

Introduction

This book is about creativity and creative probem solving. Specifically, it explains how to get ideas using a variety of idea generation methods I call "brain boosters." The helpful thing about brain boosters is that they increase your options. Options can give you more control over your life, reduce uncertainty, and make it easier to achieve your goals.

Brain Boosters for Business Advantage describes 101 brain boosters, which includes every significant formal idea generation method developed to date. In some respects, it is similar to my earlier book, *Techniques of Structured Problem Solving,* 2nd ed. (1988). However, *Brain Boosters for Business Advantage* differs substantially from my previous book in three ways: (1) it consists entirely of idea generation methods, (2) it is more readable and useful for everyday needs, and (3) it has a more hands-on approach, with considerably more examples of how to use the boosters.

Although brain boosters can be used to stimulate everyday creativity, this book was written specifically with the business person in mind. Whether your field is new product development, marketing, research and development, finance, human resources, or manufacturing, *Brain Boosters for Business Advantage* is an indispensable aid for sparking new ideas and making you more competitive.

Brain Boosters for Business Advantage has twelve chapters and is divided into three parts. Part 1 contains explanatory background material on how to use the boosters. Part 2 describes boosters for individuals, and Part 3 contains boosters designed especially for groups.

Part 1, "Getting Started," contains three chapters that explain the importance of brain boosters and their relation to problem solving, the necessity of developing a creative atmosphere when generating ideas, and different classifications of the boosters. Chapter 1 introduces the topics of problems and problem solving with an emphasis on the importance of creativity—and brain boosters—in business. Chapter 2 looks at major creative-thinking principles such as the need to defer judgment and test assumptions. These principles are essential if you want to benefit fully from the boosters. Finally, Chapter 3 describes how the boosters are organized in this book and provides a short primer on how to use them effectively.

Part 2, "Individual Brain Boosters," focuses on individual brain boosters and has five chapters. Chapter 4, "No-Brainers," looks at techniques that are relatively easy to implement and don't involve much preparation. Chapter 5, "Ticklers," describes methods that rely on various forms of stimuli to prompt ideas, and Chapter 6, "Combinations," concentrates on boosters that combine stimuli that may be either related or unrelated to the problem. Chapter 7, "Blue Skies," focuses on boosters that are based on free association (that is, one idea or stimulus leads to another, which leads to another, and so forth). Chapter 8, "Grab Bag," represents miscellaneous techniques involving analogies and reversals. All the boosters in Part 2 can also be adapted for group use.

Part 3, "Group Brain Boosters," is devoted to group brain boosters and contains the final four chapters of the book. Chapters 9 and 10 describe brainstorming boosters that use either related stimuli (Chapter 9) or unrelated stimuli (Chapter 10). Chapters 11 and 12 describe boosters that involve a procedure known as "brainwriting"— the silent generation of ideas in a group setting. The boosters in Chapter 11 generate ideas using related stimuli, and the boosters in Chapter 12 use unrelated stimuli.

I encourage you to try a variety of boosters and discover which ones work best for you. That's the advantage of having such a large number of choices. You'll probably find that some boosters will work better than others with specific types of problems. There's no such thing as the best booster, although we all have preferences. Approach the boosters as you would new ideas: Give them a chance and they may reward you.

PART

1

GETTING
STARTED

The Introduction explains how this book is organized so, if you've not already done so, you are encouraged to read it.

Part 1 examines how to

- ♥ Use brain boosters for problem solving

- ♥ Develop a creative atmosphere when generating ideas

- ♥ Use the different classifications of brain boosters effectively

The three chapters in Part 1 provide the foundation you'll need to understand how brain boosters work. The boosters will work just fine without this material. However, you'll find the boosters more beneficial if you have a basic understanding of creative thinking principles, the nature of problems and problem solving, and the different types of boosters.

Chapter 1 provides a brief overview of the general nature of problems and the importance of creativity in business.

Chapter 2 focuses on basic creative thinking principles that are fundamental to benefiting from the boosters. For instance, you'll read about the importance of separating idea generation from idea evaluation and of avoiding negative thinking. You'll also learn about the need to create new problem perspectives—a basic mechanism of all brain boosters.

Chapter 3 categorizes the boosters based on how they work. For instance, two types of boosters designed for individuals are "ticklers," which use stimuli related or unrelated to the problem to trigger ideas, and "combinations," which combine related or unrelated stimuli to generate ideas. Once you learn and experience how the boosters work, you'll be amazed at how easy it is to create hundreds of ideas.

CHAPTER
1

Creativity—That's the Problem

We live in a world of turbulent change. New data. New people. New technology. New problems. We are bombarded every day with something new. Realities shift faster than we can deal with them. What we like today we may only tolerate tomorrow. We need a program to tell the good guys from the bad guys.

In this turbulent world, traditional problem-solving methods are no longer effective in all situations. What worked yesterday may not apply today. Change has increased at such an accelerated, dizzying pace that it's difficult to tell if you are on or off the merry-go-round. Routine, analytical approaches—the ideal of the Industrial Age—rarely work in all situations. Bureaucracy and standardization are no longer reliable crutches. Instead, we now must look for new ways to cope. New ways to deal with new data, new people, new technology, new problems.

Creative Solutions

To cope with change, you need creative solutions you can customize to fit any situation, solutions designed for your special needs. What works for you, however, may not work for someone else, and vice versa. Your solutions must be tailored to your situations or you may not resolve your problems. *Adaptability* and *flexibility* are key words in our changing world.

This emphasis on customization and personalization may be here sooner than you think. Scientists at such organizations as MIT's Media Lab have been working on ways to merge technology such as computers, televisions, and newspapers. As technologies merge, customized information dispensers may result. An example would be electronic newspapers customized to your preferences for stories and features. This emphasis on customization highlights the emerging trend of discarding routine, outdated, and standardized organizational structures.

Flexible Responses to Change

Rapidly changing environments with complex and diverse elements require flexible and innovative responses. Rigid operating systems are ineffective in such environments. Flexible systems, in contrast, are characterized by multiple solution possibilities. Creative solutions can provide flexibility by increasing your options and helping you cope and adapt. The more ideas you have, the more solution avenues will be at your disposal. New ideas can open up new worlds, new insights, and new ways of doing old things. Creativity, in short, can help you reinvent yourself and your organization.

Michael Hammer and James Champy illustrate the importance of flexibility in their best-selling book, *Reengineering the Corporation*. The authors define reengineering simply as starting over. To start over, companies must test assumptions about organizational processes and devise new ways of doing things. In effect, there must be a "defeat of habit" as George Lois notes in his quotation at the beginning of this chapter. These new beginnings, however, require new ideas and new ways of looking at things—in effect, creative perspectives.

Using Creativity Techniques

Businesses need creative perspectives and solutions to conceive new product and process ideas, marketing strategies, and ways of allocating and using resources. Creativity is the magic word that can turn around your company, division, or department.

Many companies, such as 3M, Frito-Lay, and Texas Instruments, have introduced systematic creativity methods into their training and processes with outstanding results. Frito-Lay, for instance, reports documented cost savings over a four-year period of almost $600 million due to their creativity training programs. Although you may not achieve such spectacular outcomes, you can improve your current products, programs, and processes more dramatically than you ever imagined.

There is nothing magical about creativity; it's just a matter of applying the right attitude and technology in a climate receptive to creative thinking and new ideas. The technology of creativity techniques can multiply and magnify human brainpower in organizations. Unfortunately, much of this brainpower is typically underused and underappreciated. We often take our most important and useful resources for granted. Whether because of familiarity or simply lack of awareness, we fail to harness creative minds. Or when we do use this brainpower, we lack the techniques to leverage the mind's full potential—whether working alone or in groups.

Generating Creative Ideas

Many of us don't have the resources or abilities to generate the creative ideas we need. This is especially true in the business world with its complex, ever-changing environments. Competitive pressures require faster delivery of new products and services. In short, businesses are pushed to innovate before the competition does. Failure to do so can yield even fewer creative responses—and less financial profit.

The traditional approach of leaving innovation to chance is no longer effective in a world of

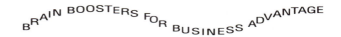

global politics, a changing labor force, rapid technological advances, and economic uncertainties. Tried-and-true idea generation methods have also lost their potency. Companies can't count on internal "creatives" to solve all their problems, and even traditional group idea generation has its weaknesses. Brainstorming, as practiced in most organizations, is about as effective as consulting a Ouija board. Even experienced brainstorming groups find that the well runs dry after interacting with the same people year after year.

Most individuals and groups in organizations occasionally need a brainpower boost to achieve "home run" or breakthrough ideas. They can't rely on traditional brainstorming. They need a number of methods in their idea toolkits. The more methods they can employ, the greater the odds of producing a hot idea.

The following chapters describe and discuss 101 proven brain boosters (idea generation methods) for individuals and groups. You probably won't use all these methods; instead, you will focus on a few of your favorites. If you generate ideas in groups on a regular basis, you will appreciate the number and diversity of methods. Whenever the well runs dry, you can simply try another method.

Defining Problems

Before generating ideas, you first need to understand more about problems. One general definition describes a problem in terms of some difficult obstacle or goal. According to this definition, anything difficult to overcome is a problem. Although this definition is descriptive, it is not precise enough for most purposes.

Deviation From the Standard

Kepner and Tregoe (1981) provide another definition of a problem: "a deviation from an expected standard of performance." This definition is more descriptive for general use. If you need to determine the cause of a problem, then this is an excellent definition. Day-to-day idea generation, however, is not especially concerned with problem causes. Although determining causes may be important as part of the overall creative problem-solving process, such determinations are not useful for pure idea generation.

Kepner and Tregoe's definition is essentially *convergent* in that problem solvers attempt to converge on a cause by eliminating various alternative explanations. Idea generation, in contrast, is more *divergent*—problem solvers attempt to generate many different alternatives. In the case of idea generation, however, alternatives are solutions and not explanations. Because the idea generation methods in this book are divergent, Kepner and Tregoe's definition doesn't fit.

BRAIN BOOSTERS FOR BUSINESS ADVANTAGE

A Gap Between the Real and the Ideal

MacCrimmon and Taylor (1976) propose another definition that is more appropriate for our purposes. They define a problem as a gap between a current and a desired state of affairs—that is, a gap between where you are and where you would like to be. An example might be when you are dissatisfied with the brand position of one of your products and wish the product were more competitive. If you perceive things that way, you have a problem. If you are unaware of your competitive position or there is nothing you can do about it, however, then perhaps you don't have a problem. It's all relative.

Tackling the Challenge

Most problems also involve some uncertainty and present a challenge. They can be trouble, right here in River City. You want to do something about them, but you don't know exactly what.

The type of problem you face will determine how to resolve it. For instance, if your car runs out of gas, you have a problem. The solution in this case is relatively simple: put in more gas. 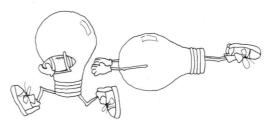 Any other solution would be a waste of time (unless gas was not available). You don't need to spend a lot of energy and effort being creative unnecessarily.

What Type of Problem Do You Have?

Most problems can be categorized according to how much structure they possess. For instance, if your problem is well structured, you would have a clear idea of how to solve it. The previous problem, running out of gas, is clearly a well-structured problem.

On the other hand, some problems are more fuzzy and less clearly structured. They provide relatively little guidance. An example would be a problem of generating new product ideas. In this case, there are many possible options but no clear-cut way to proceed (that is, no way that will guarantee a new product home run).

The type of problem will determine the approach to use. In general, you should hope that all of your problems are well structured. According to Nobel Prize winner Herbert Simon (1977), the goal of all problem solving is to make problems well structured. Such problems are the easiest to solve, because you can use a routine response. Fuzzy problems with less structure require a creative response. For these problems, you must devise custom-made responses that require more time and effort. This book provides techniques to help you with problems that aren't well structured.

Problem Solving

If you accept a problem as a gap between a current and a desired state, then problem solving can be defined as the process of making something into what you want it to be. That is, when you solve a problem, you transform "what is" into "what should be." This means you have to figure out how to do something different. You have to change the status quo into another status. How you do this is the trick.

The more ideas you generate, the closer you will come to transforming an existing problem state into a desired one. For instance, suppose you currently possess a 12 percent market share of a product line and your objective is to capture a 15 percent share. If so, you will need options to reduce the 3 percent gap. Every idea you generate increases the overall probability of reducing this gap and achieving your goal. The more ideas you can spew out, the easier it will be to resolve your problem. Thus, the more techniques you have at your disposal, the easier it will be to do problem solving.

Creativity and Serendipity

There is only one way in which a person acquires a new idea: by the combination or

*association of two or more ideas he already
has into a new juxtaposition in such a manner
as to discover a relationship among them of
which he was not previously aware.*

Francis A. Cartier

Many people don't understand the importance of having a variety of techniques in their "problem-solving kits." It is true, as Francis Cartier notes, that new ideas do result from combining previous ideas. However, the process involved in producing new insights is not so simple. New ideas can be generated by combining ideas discovered by chance or by searching more systematically.

Serendipitous Discoveries

There is nothing wrong with serendipity, of course. The world today would not be the same without it. The history of science, for example, is full of stories about how new ideas came about through chance. Take rooster sperm...please. It may seem odd, but rooster sperm illustrates the importance of the ability to recognize a creative idea when it presents itself. Rooster sperm has been responsible indirectly for providing sight to many people, but the creative insight involved might never have been discovered had it not been for a series of accidental happenings.

It all started in a laboratory outside London, England, right after World War II. Scientists were experimenting with fructose as a fowl sperm preservative. Their supply of fructose was kept in a cold room the scientists shared with another laboratory located about five miles away. One day, one of the scientists entered the supply room to retrieve a bottle of fructose, picked up a bottle without a label, and used the contents inside. Eureka! The contents of the bottle successfully preserved the sperm.

It turned out that the bottle with no label actually belonged to the other lab, and the bottle contained glycerin, not fructose. Thus, serendipity played a role in solving a scientific problem. But wait. There's more! The sequel to this story is that years later, a scientist working on organ transplants remembered the rooster experiments and the preservative powers of glycerin. His problem involved preserving human corneas for transplantation. Glycerin provided just what he needed. As a result, more people can see thanks to that bottle with the missing label.

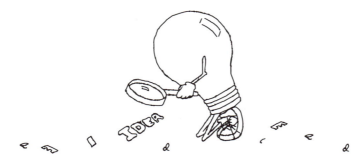

Searching for Solutions

The fowl sperm story illustrates more than the need for patience to allow creative solutions to emerge. Patience is important, as is the need to capitalize on chance events. A trained, knowledgeable mind is required to recognize when combinations of events or elements suggest something new. However, today's fast-changing, competitive business environment doesn't provide the luxury of waiting for serendipity, even for the most skilled business mind. Rather, the business world needs a way to search systematically for solutions. That's where this book can help.

Become familiar with the techniques in this book and you'll always have a powerful resource at your disposal. With the variety of methods described, you should never run out of ideas. And, most importantly, you should never have to rely on serendipity for all of your best ideas.

CHAPTER
2

Creativity Principles

When in doubt, make a fool of yourself. There is a microscopically thin line between being brilliantly creative and acting like the most gigantic idiot on earth. So what the hell, leap.

Cynthia Heimel

The brain boosters in this book will help you generate lots of ideas. There's no question about that. Brain boosters can't do it all for you, however. They are just tools to help express your innate creative potential. To produce a lot of hot ideas, you need the proper frame of mind and a variety of stimuli to energize your creative brainpower. (If you want to get on with generating ideas, skip ahead to Chapter 4.)

To use and maintain this frame of mind, you'll need to understand a few basic creative thinking principles. These principles make up the attitudinal and psychological foundation of all brain boosters. You'll understand your problems better if you can think more creatively, and you'll generate higher-quality ideas when you apply the principles of creative thinking. However, really good creative thinking is neither simple nor easy. Therefore, the more you know about thinking creatively, the easier it will be.

Your mind is a reservoir of ideas. What you know is the sum total of all you have experienced and learned. The ideas are in there; all you have to do is get them out. However, you'll never tap all the ideas inside without the proper mental attitude and approach. There's no way you can recall everything. Moreover, you'll never think of certain ideas unless you rely on different sources of stimulation. Your mind is a free association tool as much as it is a database of ideas.

Fortunately, you don't have to recall everything to think creatively. All you have to do is combine your innate creativity with brain boosters (stimulation sources) and creative thinking principles. Your knowledge and experience will then help you generate the associations that lead to ideas.

This chapter looks at a few major principles of creative thinking. If you apply them when problem solving, there is no guarantee that workable solutions will result. You will, however, increase the odds that you'll be able to think of more and higher quality ideas.

We will look at six major creative thinking principles in this chapter:

❶ Separate idea generation from evaluation.

❷ Test assumptions.

❸ Avoid patterned thinking.

❹ Create new perspectives.

❺ Minimize negative thinking.

❻ Take prudent risks.

Separating Idea Generation From Evaluation

If you don't remember anything else from this chapter, remember this: when you generate ideas, separate generation from evaluation. This is the most important creative thinking principle.

You'll never achieve your full creative potential until you apply this principle every time you generate ideas. The reason is simple: creative problem solving requires both divergent and convergent thinking. Idea generation is *divergent*—you want to get as many ideas as possible; idea evaluation is *convergent*—you want to narrow down the pool of ideas and select the best ones. If you try to do both activities at once, you won't do either one well.

Effective problem solvers have learned to separate these two activities; that is, first they generate ideas and then they evaluate them. But average problem solvers use a sequential approach instead: generate-evaluate-generate-evaluate-generate, and so forth. These problem solvers commingle generation and evaluation. They rarely move on to think about another idea until they have analyzed the previous idea in all possible ways. The result is a limited number of overanalyzed ideas.

For many people, such mixing may seem natural. They may use this method frequently because it is what they have always done. There is one thing wrong with this system, however: it is the worst way to generate ideas. Commingling generation and evaluation usually yields few ideas. It also creates a negative climate that is not conducive to creative thinking.

Before beginning any idea generation session—whether by yourself or in a group—remind yourself or others that the best way to get ideas is to defer judgment. Save the analysis and critical thinking for later, after you have generated all the ideas you can. Then and only then will it be time to evaluate the ideas.

Testing Assumptions

Testing assumptions is probably the second most important creative thinking principle, because it is the basis for all creative perceptions. You see only what you think you see. Whenever you look at something, you make assumptions about reality. Optical illusions—one form of creative perception—depend on this phenomenon.

Most psychology students, for instance, are familiar with the picture that combines an old and

a young woman (see Figure 2-1). Which of the two women you see depends on how you look at the picture, and how you look at the picture depends on the assumptions you make about the stimulus elements in the picture (that is, the lines and their relationship to one another). If you assume one configuration of lines, you see the old woman; if you assume another configuration, you see the young woman.

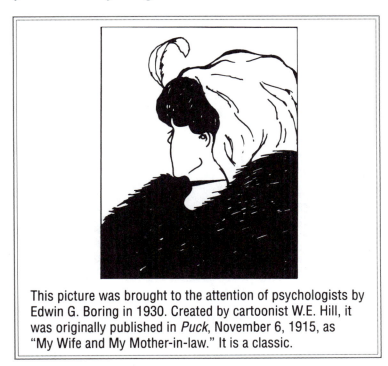

This picture was brought to the attention of psychologists by Edwin G. Boring in 1930. Created by cartoonist W.E. Hill, it was originally published in *Puck*, November 6, 1915, as "My Wife and My Mother-in-law." It is a classic.

Figure 2-1. Young/Old Woman

In one sense, optical illusions cause you to see one thing when something else may also be present. In a similar manner, we respond differently when confronted with different stimuli. You may look at a flower and feel happy because it reminds you of a loving relationship; someone else, however, may look at the same flower and feel sad because it reminds her of the recent death of a loved one. Both people in this example perceive the flower, but they also "see" the qualities of either happiness or sadness. To know why they see these qualities, they must test assumptions.

The same principle holds true when using brain boosters to generate ideas. Brain boosters present stimuli that elicit certain responses. Your particular response will depend on the assumptions you make about a particular stimulus. The more stimuli you use, the greater the potential idea pool. When these stimuli and different individual reactions are used in a group, the potential quantity and quality of ideas is increased. More stimuli and more people yield more assumptions, which in turn yield more ideas. More ideas give you more options and more chances to resolve your problems.

Everyday Assumptions

You can't be an effective problem solver unless you know how to test assumptions. Unfortunately, most of us aren't very good at this. Every day we act before thinking through what we are doing or the possible consequences. In fact, we make so many daily decisions that it is impossible to test all the potential assumptions.

For instance, the simple act of talking with someone else involves many assumptions. You must assume that the other person actually heard what you said and understood you, that the person's nonverbal reactions indicate what you think they indicate, and that you can figure out any hidden meanings or purposes.

Breakthrough Solutions

Another reason testing assumptions is important is that it can yield perceptual breakthroughs. Testing assumptions can help you shift perspectives and view problems in a new light. As the philosopher Marcel Proust once said, "The real voyage of discovery consists not in seeking new lands, but in seeking with new eyes." The result often is a breakthrough solution or, at the least, a new problem definition. There is an old joke that illustrates this point nicely:

> Two men were camping in the wilderness when they were awakened one morning by a large bear rummaging through their food supply. The bear noticed the men and started lumbering toward them.
>
> The men still were in their sleeping bags and didn't have time to put on their boots, so they picked up their boots and began running away from the bear. The terrain was very rough, however, and they couldn't make much progress. The bear was gaining on them.
>
> Suddenly, one of the men sat down and began pulling on his boots. His friend couldn't believe what he was seeing and said, "Are you nuts? Can't you see that the bear is almost here? Let's go!"

The man on the ground continued putting on his boots. As he did this, he looked up at the other man and said, "Well, Charlie, the way I look at it, I don't have to outrun the bear—I only have to outrun you!"

And so, another problem is resolved by testing assumptions. In this case, both men originally assumed the problem was how to outrun the bear. When one of the men tested this assumption, a creative solution popped out. This single act provided that man with one critical extra option. His spontaneous creative thinking enabled him to gain an edge over his "competitor."

How to Test Assumptions

If you are in business, this may all sound familiar. Sometimes all it takes is one extra option to give you an edge over your competitor. In addition to

using the brain boosters described in this book, you can get that competitive edge by testing problem assumptions. Of course, you can't test assumptions about every problem. You can test assumptions, however, about problems of strategic importance or problems with potentially serious consequences. The lesson, then, is be selective.

So how do you test assumptions? The answer is provided by Albert Einstein: "The important thing is to never stop questioning." Ask a lot of questions about whatever problem you're trying to resolve. The more questions you ask, the closer you'll get to understanding your problem.

One way to enhance the questioning process is to use the basic journalism "five w" questions of who, what, where, when, and why. These questions can help you seek data more efficiently. For instance, you might ask the following questions: Who is the competition? Who are the customers? What does your company do? What is your mission? Where can you make improvements? Where can you get data about your competition? When should you enter a new market? When are your customers most likely to buy your products? Why do people buy your products? Why do you want to enter a new market?

Ask lots of questions and you'll understand your business better. If you have a better understanding of your business, you'll get more creative insights on how to improve it. It's as simple as that.

Avoiding Patterned Thinking

Try this little exercise: Fold your arms the way you normally would cross them. Notice which hands are on top of your arms. For instance, my left arm lies across my right arm. Now quickly reverse this position (in my case, my right arm should lie across my left). You'll probably notice that the second position is more difficult. It's not "natural."

Here's another, similar exercise: Interlock your fingers in the way most comfortable for you. Either your right or left index finger should be on top. Reverse your fingers so the opposite finger is on top. Not so easy, is it? We all have certain patterns of behaving and thinking which impede our creative thinking.

Habit-bound Thinking

What you have just experienced is habit-bound behavior. We all have a comfortable, secure way of doing things, and there's nothing wrong with that. A little security can't hurt.

A problem occurs, however, whenever we try to break out of a rut. The very thought of doing something different can be terrifying. Yet, creative thinking frequently requires that we do just that. As Charles Kettering, inventor of the electric automobile starter, once noted, "You'll never get the view from the bottom of a rut."

Let's try a couple more exercises to illustrate habit-bound thinking: First, repeat the word "joke" three times. Now, quickly, what is the white of an egg called?

Here's another: What word is formed by adding one letter to the following? __ANY. Very good! Now, what word is formed by adding one letter to the following? __ENY.

Most people who respond to the first exercise say "yolk." Of course, this is incorrect. By having you repeat the word "joke," I established a pattern involving the "oak" sound. To solve the problem, however, you have to break away from the pattern and focus on the correct answer: albumen.

The most common response to the first word in the second exercise is the word "many" (a few independent thinkers may say "zany" and mess up the demonstration). The "many" response then establishes a pattern with the sound of just one word and makes it more difficult to think of the second word, "deny."

Breaking Out of the Rut

All these exercises illustrate how difficult it can be to do something different. We become so accustomed to doing things a certain way that we may lose the ability to break away.

So what can you do? Perhaps the most important thing is to increase your awareness of how everyone is a victim of patterned thinking. Once you do this, you'll be more aware of when you are caught in a rut. Beyond simple awareness, however, you also can break away with some practice.

Familiarity is the handmaiden of habit. We sometimes become so familiar with things that we aren't even aware of it. For instance, try to draw the face of your watch in detail without looking at it. (Many people add numbers that don't even exist.) Or the next time you drive to work, notice something you've never seen before. After a few mornings of this activity, you'll be surprised at all you see.

To break out of patterns, you must make a conscious effort. First become more aware of your habit-bound thinking; then deliberately practice changing it.

Creating New Perspectives

When I have arranged a bouquet for the purpose of painting it, I always turn to the side I did not plan.

Pierre Auguste Renoir

When the impressionist painter Renoir made this statement, he suggested the importance of developing creative perspectives. It could be argued that there can be no creative product without a creative perspective. To produce something new, you must see something new. What you see may be some previously overlooked element of a problem or a solution from combining two previously unjoined problem elements or ideas.

Two Insightful Thinkers

Perhaps the most well-known historical example of a sudden insight involves Archimedes, who jumped out of his bathtub and ran naked through the streets, shouting, "Eureka! Eureka!" This rather odd behavior followed his discovery of the principle of displacement. While taking a bath, he noticed how his body weight displaced an equal amount of water. This led him to an insight, or new perspective.

A more contemporary example is Art Fry, inventor of Post-it Notes. He combined his need for a piece of paper that would stay put when he marked his church hymns with a scrap of paper that used a "failed" glue developed by Spencer Silver, one of his colleagues at 3M Company. Both Archimedes and Art Fry produced a more creative perspective when they combined two previously unconnected problem elements.

Keeping Sight of the Big Picture

Not everyone can make creative connections easily. We sometimes get so close to a problem that we lose ourselves in it— something like the old expression "You can't see the forest for the trees."

In one respect, becoming deeply involved with a problem automatically increases our understanding of it. This is good. We must understand problems to deal with them.

Too much understanding, however, can be harmful because it causes us to narrow our focus and lose a broader perspective. This is bad. Too much detailed problem awareness causes us to lose sight of the big picture. The solution: create new perspectives.

Each brain booster in this book will help you produce new perspectives and see problems with new eyes. Boosters do this by facilitating free association, combining problem elements, promoting interaction with other people, or eliciting responses to various stimuli. In each case, the outcome is the same: new ways of thinking about a problem. Over time, you'll find that the more you use a variety of brain boosters, the easier it will become to create new perspectives.

Minimizing Negative Thinking

Unless you are an exceptional person, you are a natural critic. From an early age you have learned to analyze and criticize anything new. Now that you are an adult, being critical is second nature. You are an expert at it.

What is your typical first reaction when someone proposes a new idea? Do you usually say something like "That's fantastic," "That's a great idea," or "That's really interesting"? Probably not.

Although there may be a few exceptions, most of us come preprogrammed with the "automatic no" response. Through training and conditioning in school and at home, we have learned to criticize first and think later. It's almost as if we have learned that it is better to reject something new outright than even to consider its potential value as a solution.

An Exercise in Negative Thinking

To illustrate this automatic no tendency, here's a little exercise: Take five minutes and write down every negative response you can think of to a new idea. When you finish, compare your list with the following one. Chances are there are a lot of similarities, if not direct duplications.

- Our problem is different.
- We tried that once before.
- We don't have enough time.
- We don't have enough help.
- Our system is too small for this.
- We've always done it this way.
- Our present method is time-tested and reliable.
- It's impractical.
- It's ahead of its time.

- It's behind the times.

- We're not ready for it yet.

- We've had too much of this lately.

- You can't teach an old dog new tricks.

- Our young, progressive group doesn't need it.

- It will require a heavy investment.

- It will never pay for itself.

- If no investment is required, how do you expect it to work?

- It's too radical.

- It's almost the same as what we're doing now.

- It looks good on paper, but it won't work.

- It violates professional standards.

- The board won't like it.

- It's outside my scope of responsibility.

- It conflicts with policy.

- The present method is working. Why rock the boat?

You probably could think of many more examples with very little effort. Now, what would happen if you tried to make a list of positive responses? Try it. Take five minutes and write down every positive response you can think of to a new idea. Most likely, this second list will be shorter than the first. It's much more difficult to think of positive responses.

Developing Balanced Responses

To break out of the negative thinking groove, you'll need to develop more balanced responses to new ideas. There are a number of ways to do this. Here are three approaches:

❶ Try viewing ideas as raw materials; that is, initial ideas are the fragile creatures we often transform into more workable solutions. So be gentle. Support and cradle all new ideas—these newborns (as professional inventor Doug Hall calls them) frequently can be modified or can help stimulate improved versions.

❷ Every time you hear a new idea, train yourself to think or say, "What's good about it? What is at least one positive feature of that idea?" If you can think of one positive aspect, then you will benefit from what may initially have appeared useless. Moreover, the positive feature may stimulate a better idea.

❸ Use a balanced response to new ideas. Say (or think) what you like about the idea, what you find interesting about it, and then what you dislike. This will help prevent the negative climate in individuals and groups that often accompanies responses to ideas.

Taking Prudent Risks

A failure is an opportunity to start over again, but more intelligently.

Henry Ford

You can't be a creative thinker unless you are a failure. No one ever truly succeeds without failing first. For instance, novelist John Creasey got 753 rejection slips before he published 564 books. Sports fans know that Babe Ruth struck out 1,330 times—a pretty poor record. Fortunately, he also hit 714 home runs. And R.H. Macy failed seven times before his New York store caught on.

Creative thinking involves a certain amount of risk taking. Many people fear risks, however, because risks can lead to failure. And who wants to be branded a failure? Yet we must take risks to have any chance to succeed. An old quotation describes this philosophy perfectly:

To laugh is to risk appearing the fool.

To place your ideas, your dreams, before a crowd is to risk their loss.

To live is to risk dying.

To hope is to risk despair.

To try is to risk failure.

The person who risks nothing, does nothing, and is nothing.

Only a person who risks is free.

Anonymous

Not all risks are equal. Some risks are more serious than others. For instance, the potential risks of idea generation are much less serious than the risks of implementation. Every time we think of or suggest an idea, we take a risk. Because we can't survive without new ideas, we must constantly take such risks.

The likely negative consequences of suggesting a "stupid" idea, however, pale in comparison with the risks of implementing an idea. Introducing a product that later fails will cost a company much more than any embarrassment someone might experience from suggesting a so-called stupid idea. Lose face and the company goes on to play another day; lose too much market share and the game may soon be over.

Viewed this way, risk taking isn't so bad. Because brain boosters involve risks of generation and not implementation, force yourself to be willing to suggest whatever ideas pop up. Remember, ideas are the raw material of solutions and not the final product. Initial ideas have the potential to spark more practical solutions. They don't all have to be winners. Adopt this philosophy and you'll remove a lot of pressure when using brain boosters.

CHAPTER
3

A Short Primer on Brain Booster Techniques

You have learned about the importance of creativity and types of problems (Chapter 1), as well as major creative thinking principles (Chapter 2). Now it's time to get down to business and generate some ideas.

Before looking at the brain boosters, however, you first need to understand more about how idea generation techniques work. This knowledge should make it easier to use the brain boosters and increase your understanding about creative thinking in general. If you don't think you need this information, move on to the next chapter.

To begin, take a few minutes and think of different uses for a coffee mug. That's right—a coffee mug. Think of as many uses as you can.

Are you finished? How many ideas did you generate? Two? Four? Six? Eight? That's not enough. Try to think of a few more.

Next, look over your list and see if your ideas fall into categories. For instance, do some of your ideas involve uses for holding foods and non-foods? Or did you think of giving mugs away as presents or awards for different events? Or you might even have thought of building things with them (for example, a coffee cup castle). Your ideas should fall into several categories. Now use these categories to think of more ideas. Good job! That's enough.

We often use categories to stimulate ideas because they can help stretch our thinking. Unfortunately, many of us use only a limited number of categories, or we use rather conventional categories. If you really stretched your thinking, however, you might have broken away from conventional categories. You might have thought of some offbeat uses that involved crushing or otherwise altering the cups. For instance, you could remove the cup handles and use them as handles for kitchen cupboards, or you could crush the cups and use the remains for automobile tire traction on ice.

Here's an innovative use for a coffee cup that you probably didn't think of: Teresa Smith, manager of a Taco Mayo in Oklahoma City, was depositing the store's evening receipts in a bank's night depository. A man ran up and grabbed the restaurant's money bag from her purse. She poured a cup of hot coffee on him and then hit him on the head with the cup. The man turned and ran with the money, but also with an injured head. Perhaps he'll think twice now before he robs a coffee-mug-toting woman!

This exercise may have helped you think of many more ideas than you thought you could. The categories helped target your thinking and allowed you to search for ideas more systematically. All it took was a different way to conduct your idea search. The brain boosters in the following chapters do the same thing. They help you draw out more ideas than if you were thinking unaided. And although a group will produce more ideas than an individual will, the brain booster techniques will even help groups surpass their collective brain power.

Technique Types

There are a number of ways to classify idea generation methods. The two most common are as *individual* and *group* procedures. However, this distinction is not clear-cut, because groups can use all of the individual brain boosters, but individuals cannot use all of the group brain boosters. Some of the group brain boosters were designed specifically with groups in mind. For instance, some group boosters involve passing idea cards from one person to another. (You could try this as an individual, but you would probably feel a little silly!)

You should follow one basic rule whether you are using individual or group brain boosters:

DEFER ALL JUDGMENT WHEN GENERATING IDEAS.

This rule is so important, I'd like to repeat it:

DEFER ALL JUDGMENT WHEN GENERATING IDEAS.

You must abide by this rule if you want to generate many different ideas. The more ideas you list, the greater are the odds that one will resolve your problem. You won't produce many ideas if you spend time criticizing and evaluating them. Save the evaluation for later, after you have listed all the ideas you can. Remember: No evaluation with generation. (Repeat five times.)

Individual Brain Boosters

Individual brain boosters can be classified in several ways. After reviewing the available techniques, I settled on five (booster numbers for the individual techniques are in brackets):

❶ No-brainers (Chapter 4) require relatively little effort. An example would be the coffee cup exercise. Asking a friend for an idea (Brain Borrow [2]) is another example.

➋ *Ticklers* (Chapter 5) generate ideas by providing some sort of stimulus for you to play against. Examples include various pictures (Picture Tickler [17]), words (PICLed Brains [16]), and objects (Tickler Things [21]). You can examine these stimuli and see what associations develop.

➌ *Combinations* (Chapter 6) blend or compare different problem elements and use the combinations and juxtapositions to prompt ideas. Examples include Combo Chatter [24], Noun Action [28], and Parts Is Parts [30].

➍ *Blue skies* methods (Chapter 7) rely more on free association to stimulate creative thinking. An example would be using the words "what if" to help inspire ideas (What if...? [49]). Or you might use exaggeration (Exaggerate That [39]) to help stretch your thinking.

➎ *Grab bag* methods (Chapter 8) represent a miscellaneous category containing two types of techniques: *backward* and *just alike only different*. Backward methods reverse some aspect of a problem to produce a different perspective and, it is hoped, new ideas. Thus, you might reverse assumptions about a problem (Turn Around [52]) and use the reversals as stimulators. Just alike only different procedures use analogies to generate ideas. Two examples are Bionic Ideas [53] and Chain Alike [54].

As I mentioned, most of these brain boosters were not developed with groups in mind. However, it is easy to adapt them for small groups. Just explain the basic procedures involved and get on with it. (And don't forget to defer judgment!)

Group Brain Boosters

Before learning about group brain boosters, you need to know a little about how to work with groups to generate ideas. Here are some points to keep in mind:

- Use groups of about five people. Research has consistently shown that this is the optimal size for problem-solving groups. Four will often work well in trained groups or groups with a skilled facilitator. In a pinch, groups of six will work under the same conditions.

- Make sure all groups understand the basic ground rule of deferring judgment. Encourage them to reinforce this rule as they interact with each other.

- Try to create a fun environment. Encourage playfulness and humor. Research shows that groups characterized by laughter and humor tend to generate more ideas than their less humorous and playful counterparts.

- Use as many brain boosters as you can in the time available. Different boosters can spark different ideas depending on the personalities and experiences of the group members. What works in one group may fizzle in another. I can still remember a group member telling me that a certain technique wasn't any good and that I should stop using it. Later that day, a member of another group remarked to me that the same technique was one of the best he ever had used. Go figure.

Brainstorming and Brainwriting

Group brain boosters can be classified as either *brainstorming* or *brainwriting*. Brainstorming, of course, refers to traditional verbal idea generation in a group. Brainwriting is a term coined in Germany that refers to the silent, written generation of ideas in a group setting.

All things being equal, brainwriting groups generate more ideas than brainstorming groups. One reason is that when we interact verbally, we are often not as productive as we might otherwise be. We criticize ideas when we shouldn't, we feel inhibited, we worry about what other people will think of our ideas, and we get sidetracked with various issues and hidden agendas. Moreover, only one person can speak at a time in brainstorming groups.

If brainwriting yields more ideas than brainstorming, why even use brainstorming groups? The answer is that we are social creatures. Most of us would have trouble not talking for a long time. We clearly can satisfy more social needs in brainstorming groups. Moreover, some brain-storming boosters provide a structure that offsets some disadvantages. Thus, if a group follows a technique's procedures as written, it should be more successful than a traditional brainstorming group with no structure.

To test these notions, I conducted an experiment using six different types of idea generation procedures. Each procedure was tested using six categories of four-person groups:

- Groups using procedure 1 generated ideas without any formal instructions.

- Groups using procedure 2 generated ideas but were instructed to follow brain-storming rules and defer judgment (as were all subsequent groups).

- Groups using procedure 3 generated ideas using one brainstorming brain booster technique (PICLed Brains [16]).

- Groups using procedure 4 generated ideas using a brainwriting procedure in which the group members didn't see one another's ideas.

- Groups using procedure 5 generated ideas using a brainwriting procedure in which the participants *did* see each other's ideas (Brain Purge [82]).

- Groups using procedure 6 generated ideas using combinations of brainstorm-ing and brainwriting methods. In addition,

each group using procedure 6 contained two skilled idea generation facilitators.

All the groups had 45 minutes to generate new snack food product ideas (which were later evaluated by a food products company). When ideas were counted, we found that the groups using procedures 1 through 5 collectively generated about 1,400 ideas, and the groups using procedure 6 generated about 1,200 ideas. In fact, groups using procedure 6 generated more than ten times as many ideas as groups using procedure 1.

To be fair, it should be noted that procedure 6 groups used Hall's (1994) Eureka! professional invention approach. The other groups were made up entirely of students with little formal brainstorming experience. When group 6 was excluded from the analysis, it was discovered that groups using procedure 5 (brainwriting while seeing one another's ideas) generated almost four times as many ideas as groups using brainstorming without instructions. There clearly are advantages to using brainstorming and brainwriting procedures (as well as skilled facilitators).

Related Versus Unrelated Stimuli

Another way to classify group techniques is according to whether the stimuli used are *related* or *unrelated* to the problem. An example of a related stimulus would be using different parts of a coffee mug to suggest ways to improve it. Most combination techniques are based on this principle. Thus, you might combine the handle with the base to spark an idea. In this case, you might think of an integrated handle and base cup warmer. You could attach different cups and the coffee would keep warm even while the cup is in your hand.

Organization of Group Techniques in This Book

The group brain boosters in this book have been organized according to whether they primarily use brainstorming or brainwriting and whether they use related or unrelated stimuli. One chapter is devoted to each group:

- Brainstorming With Related Boosters (Chapter 9)

- Brainstorming With Unrelated Boosters (Chapter 10)

- Brainwriting With Related Boosters (Chapter 11)

- Brainwriting With Unrelated Boosters (Chapter 12)

This organization of the techniques is more a matter of convenience than anything else. However, a few guidelines may help you decide which boosters to use:

- Use brainwriting boosters (Chapters 11 and 12) if (1) there are conflicts or major status differences among members of a group, or (2) there is relatively little time,

group members are inexperienced at brainstorming, and no experienced facilitator is available.

- All things being equal, use both brainstorming and brainwriting boosters.

- If you want to generate unique ideas and the group is relatively inexperienced, use boosters with unrelated stimuli (Chapters 10 and 12).

One final note: When selecting group boosters, remember that any of the individual boosters also will be appropriate for groups.

A Few of My Favorite Techniques

It is difficult to say that any one brain booster is better than another. As I indicated previously, each of us may respond differently to any given approach. What works well for you may fizzle for me. Your mood and any number of other factors may also influence your reaction.

I do, however, have my own particular favorites, which are presented in the following "Top Ten" lists. In many cases, it was almost impossible to choose among the various methods. This was especially true for the group brain boosters.

Top Ten Individual Brain Boosters

❶ Combo Chatter [24]

❷ Picture Tickler [17]

❸ I Like It Like That [55]

❹ What if...? [49]

❺ PICLed Brains [16]

❻ Turn Around [52]

❼ Exaggerate That [39]

❽ Tickler Things [21]

❾ Get Crazy [5]

❿ Word Diamond [35]

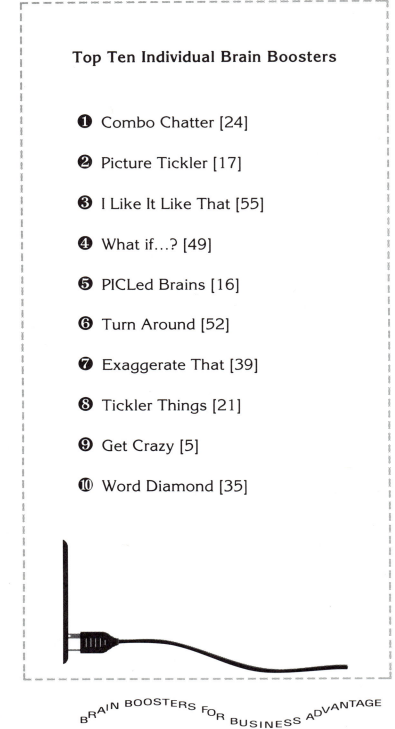

Top Ten Group Brain Boosters

❶ What's the Problem? [70]

❷ Pass the Buck [56]

❸ The Name Game [197]

❹ Brain Purge [82]

❺ Museum Madness [86]

❻ Brainsketching [94]

❼ Balloon, Balloon, Balloon [92]

❽ Brain Splitter [73]

❾ Grab Bag Forced Association [75]

❿ Pass the Hat [63]

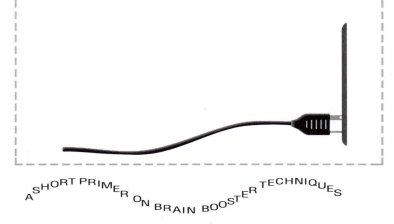

A Guide for Selecting Brain Boosters

The boosters in the Top Ten lists will help you get many ideas for a broad spectrum of problems. However, you may want more help than these lists provide. For instance, you may have specific needs for new product ideas or for ways to handle various people problems. To help you, I've put together a brain booster selection guide covering four general types of business problems: (1) strategic problems, (2) product and process problems (including new ideas and improvements on existing products or services), (3) advertising/marketing problems, and (4) people/human resource problems. This guide reflects my subjective choices of the most useful boosters. Once you experiment with different boosters, you can develop your own guide.

The lists contain only individual boosters, because group boosters provide more flexibility and discretion in terms of how group members may interact. For instance, a brainstorming group should be able to deal easily with any type of problem, depending on the composition and motivations of the members. Individual boosters, in contrast, are more structured and specific in how they can be used. This does not mean you should ignore group boosters. Consider all the group brain boosters, and in particular the "Top Ten" group boosters listed previously. One final note: Several boosters appear more than once. This simply reflects the versatility of these methods.

Boosters for Strategic Problems

If you want to generate ideas to improve strategic functioning, try the following boosters:

- Brain Mapping [36]
- Doodles [37]
- Exaggerate That [39]
- Get Crazy [5]
- I Like It Like That [55]
- Law Breaker [50]
- A Likely Story [15]
- Lotus Blossom [43]
- Mental Breakdown [7]
- PICLed Brains [16]
- Picture Tickler [17]
- Rorschach Revisionist [18]
- Say What? [19]
- Skybridging [46]
- Turn Around [52]
- We Have Met the Problem and It Is Us [48]
- What if...? [49]
- What Is It? [56]

Boosters for New Product Ideas

If your goal is to create new product ideas, try the following boosters:

- Bend It, Shape It [1]
- Brain Borrow [2]
- Chain Alike [54]
- Circle of Opportunity [23]
- Combo Chatter [24]
- Get Crazy [5]
- I Like It Like That [55]
- Law Breaker [50]
- Lotus Blossom [43]
- Parts Is Parts [30]
- PICLed Brains [16]
- Picture Tickler [17]
- Tickler Things [21]
- Turn Around [52]
- What if...? [49]

Boosters for New Product Improvements

If you want to improve existing products or processes, try the following boosters:

- Bi-Wordal [22]
- Brain Borrow [2]
- Brain Mapping [36]
- Chain Alike [54]
- Circle of Opportunity [23]
- Combo Chatter [24]
- Copy Cat [3]
- Exaggerate That [39]
- Idea Links [41]
- I Like It Like That [55]
- Idea Shopping [14]
- Ideas in a Box [25]
- Law Breaker [50]
- A Likely Story [15]
- Lotus Blossom [43]
- Mad Scientist [27]
- Parts Purge [31]
- PICLed Brains [16]
- Picture Tickler [17]

- Preppy Thoughts [32]
- Reversals [51]
- 666 [34]
- Turn Around [52]
- What if...? [49]

Boosters for Advertising/Marketing Problems

If you need to develop new ideas related to advertising or marketing problems, use the following boosters:

- A Likely Story [15]
- Brain Mapping [36]
- Copy Cat [3]
- Doodles [37]
- Exaggerate That [39]
- Excerpt Excitation [13]
- Get Crazy [5]
- Idea Shopping [14]
- Imagery Mentor [42]
- Law Breaker [50]
- Music Mania [8]
- PICLed Brains [16]

- Picture Tickler [17]
- Say Cheese [44]
- Say What? [19]
- Tabloid Tales [47]
- Text Tickler [20]
- Turn Around [52]
- What if...? [49]

Boosters for Human Resource Problems

To get ideas for problems involving people (for example, recruiting and retaining personnel, improving customer service, attracting customers), try the following boosters:

- A Likely Story [15]
- Brain Mapping [36]
- Doodles [37]
- Exaggerate That [39]
- Excerpt Excitation [13]
- I Like It Like That [15]
- Idea Diary [6]
- Imagery Mentor [42]
- Law Breaker [50]
- Mental Breakdown [7]

BRAIN BOOSTERS FOR BUSINESS ADVANTAGE

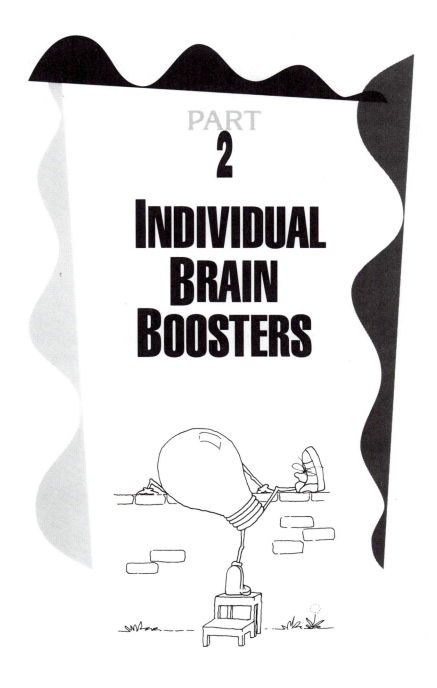

All the boosters in Part 2 were originally developed as individual idea generation aids. Individual boosters will be especially useful for people who are not comfortable working in groups or people who do most of their creative thinking alone by choice. A significant, often overlooked feature of individual boosters, however, is that they can be adapted for group use. It usually is just a simple matter of pooling the ideas of several people (four to six is about the right number of people for brainstorming ideas). Group members follow the procedure for a particular booster and brainstorm ideas as if they were working alone.

Part 2's individual brain boosters are grouped into five different categories.

- ♀ "No-brainers" are easy-to-implement idea generation procedures that require minimal effort.

- ♀ "Ticklers" are based on the principle of random stimulation.

- "Combinations" combine problem elements with different stimuli to trigger new views.

- "Blue skies" methods generate ideas using free association.

- "Grab bag" techniques represent miscellaneous boosters, including reversals and analogies.

All of these boosters are easy to use. All you have to do is try them.

C H A P T E R
4

No-Brainers

You have probably heard the expression "That's a real no-brainer!" In case you haven't, a no-brainer is an activity that requires little mental effort or ability. (It doesn't mean you don't need a brain!) No-brainer brain boosters really are "brainers" that require a little less effort and creative ability than other boosters.

Depending on your creative thinking ability, no-brainers may or may not work as well as other brain boosters. This doesn't mean they lack the potential for yielding blockbuster ideas. All brain boosters have that potential. You'll just have to experiment with brain boosters from different categories to determine the best ones for you.

1. Bend It, Shape It

This booster is quite basic. All you have to do is change a problem in different ways. It doesn't really matter what you change or how you change it. Just change it in any way possible.

If you change something, you create a new perspective, and that perspective can lead to other new perspectives and ideas. This is basic free association.

Brainstorming pioneer Alex Osborn (1963) was a master at using perspective changes to suggest new ideas. In fact, he developed a list of seventy-three idea-spurring questions designed to create new perspectives. His list included such questions as the following:

- What other product (problem) is like this one (adapt)?

- How could I change this product (modify)?

- How could I add to this product (magnify)?

- What could I take away from this product (minify)?

- What could I use instead of this product or a portion of it (substitute)?

- How could I alter this product's composition (rearrange)?

- How could I turn this problem around (reverse)?

- What could I put together to make a new product (combine)?

For instance, suppose you want to design a new, improved stapler. You might use Osborn's questions to suggest the following types of ideas:

- *Adapt:* Design a stapler that fastens without staples by pressing together sheets of paper under pressure (for example, a pair of pliers is somewhat like a stapler in that it can be used to press together things).

- *Modify:* Use bright, metallic paint.

- *Magnify:* Enlarge the stapler's top and make it ergonomic to fit a hand.

- *Minify:* Design a stapler that dispenses both small and large staples.

- *Substitute:* Make a line of staplers from different materials such as cardboard, metal, fiberglass, plastic, or polished wood.

- *Rearrange:* Design a stapler that can staple from either end.

- *Reverse:* Design a stapler that works by pulling up on a handle instead of pressing down.

- *Combine:* Design a combination stapler and magnetic paper clip dispenser.

Of course, you don't have to limit your changes to those prompted by Osborn's list. Any changes will do. You can change color, shape, smell, cost, design, texture, timing, and so forth. The possible changes are limited only by your imagination.

2. Brain Borrow

Do you sometimes feel overburdened with the responsibility for coming up with new ideas? Do you wonder how you can continue to innovate in your work or personal life? If so, you're not alone. We all occasionally experience some frustration in expressing ourselves creatively on demand. Just as we can't be all things to all people, we can't be "all ideas to all problems."

There are at least three reasons for this shortcoming. First, we are limited in how we perceive situations. We each have unique perspectives that help us generate ideas for some problems quite creatively. For other problems, however, we don't have the needed perspectives. We just can't seem to define the problem appropriately, or we make untested assumptions that constrain our creative thinking.

Second, we lack the knowledge and information needed to deal with certain problems. For instance, technical problems require specialized knowledge based on extensive formal education, training, and experience. Creativity can help only a limited amount in such situations.

Finally, we all vary in our motivations in different situations. Our individual interests dictate how motivated we will be to solve any given problem.

Thus, the issue is not whether or not you are creative. Rather, you should ask yourself whether you can bring—to this situation—the perspectives and resources needed for creative solutions. If you can't, then you have a number of options. One is to use several of the brain boosters described in this book. Another is to seek ideas from others, that is, borrow some brains. This can be accomplished in one of two ways:

❶ Consult an expert. It may turn out that you don't really need a creative solution. Instead, you may just need an already-existing solution that you didn't know existed.

But before you consult an expert, consider the nature of your problem. If it is relatively structured and closed, an expert is often the best choice; if your problem is more open-ended, an expert may have a limited range of possible solutions. That is, if your problem has just one or only a few "correct" solutions, then an expert may be your best bet.

On the other hand, if your problem has multiple solution possibilities, experts may be bound by their technical knowledge and generate only a few conventional possibilities. This is another example of why it pays to test assumptions before plunging into problem solving.

❷ If the problem is open-ended or consulting an expert is not feasible, consult several people with absolutely no knowledge of your problem. Such people can bring a fresh perspective to the problem. Unfettered by discipline-bound assumptions and logic, they can often see things we can't. Not only are they more removed from the problem, but also they are more likely to avoid preconceptions. So ask a friend, co-worker, spouse, or even a child how he or she would solve your problem.

Of course, not all the ideas you solicit from nonexperts may appear practical or workable. Remember, however, that ideas are the raw material of solutions. View the new ideas as potential solution stimulators. Examine each idea to see what more practical solution it might suggest. And modify, modify, modify. Take advantage of other people's unique perspectives and let your imagination go.

3. Copy Cat

One of the first things school children learn is "do your own work." They're also told that they'll never learn anything if they copy off of someone else. "Besides, the person you copy off of may be wrong. So keep your eyes on your own paper!"

Although this may be good advice in school, it hasn't always held up well in the business world. In fact, many businesses make a practice of copying other companies. Taken to the extreme, this practice can result in copyright and trademark violations as greedy business people try to profit from outright ripoffs. Rolex watches, for example, are frequently copied by unscrupulous companies trying to make a quick buck with an unlicensed product.

By definition, copying someone else's idea is not a creative act. There's nothing original about an idea that is exactly the same as another. Although some people argue that a product is creative if it is new to the creator, this logic loses its appeal in the business world.

If another company is already marketing an idea, you lose "creativity points" if you attempt to market the same idea. The true innovator is the

company that designed, developed, and brought to market the idea. Copy an idea and you're following the leader. Moreover, research has shown that companies that market an idea first are more likely to achieve competitive advantage and an overall greater market share.

Does the fact that copying an idea has negative consequences mean that copying is a bad business practice? The answer is yes and no. It's bad if you copy directly without permission; it's good if you use another idea only for stimulation. Copying can help if you use only a basic concept or principle from someone else's idea. That's where the Copy Cat technique comes in.

To use the Copy Cat brain booster, all you have to do is borrow the basics of another idea and adapt it to your situation. Look around to see who is doing similar things or making similar products. There doesn't have to be a direct connection. Just observe what others are doing and try to make it work for your product, process, or service.

For example, consider Kent Savage, president of Electronic Merchandising Systems, Inc., of Cincinnati, Ohio. When Savage started out in the vending machine business, he tried the conventional approach: snacks, coffee, and cold drinks. Then, six years ago, he traveled to Japan. There he saw $300 pearl necklaces and even sake offered in vending machines.

"What an eye opener," Savage now recalls. "I realized I could break out of the mold and move into higher-priced items." And so he did. When he returned to the United States, he approached Eastman Kodak and offered to sell cameras and film in his vending machines. After two years, his vending machines now sell Kodak products in more than twenty states.

In 1993, Savage introduced machines that sell tools on factory floors. His company now turns a sizable profit, with the machine tools expected to bring in more than $100 million over the next five years (some of which will come from exports to Japan, ironically).

Savage capitalized on his strengths and borrowed a concept from someone else. Once he had copied the basic idea, he turned the concept into a creative product suited for his business. Savage was a Copy Cat.

4. Dead Head Deadline

We live in a world of deadlines. Do it soon. Do it now. Do it yesterday. Just do it. It's an unrelenting pace with unrelenting deadlines. Tomorrows become todays, which become yesterdays—all too soon. If you don't do it now, you'll never do it. Deadlines are everywhere. You can't live with 'em; you can't live without 'em.

But you can use them to become more creative. Despite our lack of love for deadlines, they also have positive features. The most important of these is that deadlines provide motivation. And motivation can increase our idea productivity.

The use of deadlines is a simple, yet often overlooked, brain booster. The process involved is similar to goal setting: it gives us something to strive for and provides motivation. If we know when we have to complete a task, most of us will pace ourselves to do it. Deadlines force us to organize our thinking and move ahead.

Many of us have deadlines imposed on us. All it takes is for a boss to say, "Do such and such by tomorrow," and we'll perform. There are times, however, when we need to be creative on demand. So the next time you're stymied for a creative idea, impose a deadline on yourself. Try to think of ten more ideas by 10:00, for instance. Or decide that you will figure out how to resolve a problem by the end of the day.

Whatever deadline you establish, make sure it is realistic. Remember, however, that what is realistic is relative. It all depends on the perceiver. Thus, I might perceive a deadline of two hours as realistic, but such a time period might evoke immediate panic in someone else. If your deadline is not realistic, it won't be motivating.

5. Get Crazy

Look waaaaay down inside yourself. There are lots of hidden recesses down there, aren't there? Things known only to you and perhaps a few of your intimate friends. Things you normally don't show in polite company. That strange side only you know about. The side that views things differently.

If you look long enough, you may eventually discover the wacky you down there—the side of you that every now and then thinks of an off-the-wall idea. It's the side that makes a sudden leap of intuition, jumps to conclusions, and goes off the deep end (the side filled with clichés?). You know it's in there, so admit it. Use it occasionally to your advantage. Get crazy, get zany, get ridiculous. View your problems with new eyes.

Here's how to do it:

 Write down the most crazy, ridiculous problem solutions you can think of. The crazier the better.

❷ Forget being crazy. Zoom back to normality and get on with solving your problem. Be practical. Become the "regular" creative you.

❸ Examine each of your crazy ideas to see what more practical solution it may suggest. You may not think of one for each crazy idea, but do the best you can.

Suppose you want to convince people to buy more of your products. First, get crazy and generate some ridiculous ideas:

 Threaten people with a "long vacation" if they don't buy your products.

- Pay them $1 million for every dollar they spend on your products.

- Promise them three magic wishes.

- Attach a subliminal advertising device to their televisions.

- Have your cousin Vinnie pay them a visit.

- Send your product to every home in the world as a holiday gift and invoice the homeowners.

O.K., those are pretty ridiculous. Now, use each one to stimulate a more practical idea. Some examples:

- Offer free or partially funded vacations to people who place large orders.

- Develop a list of "magic wishes" with a lottery for customers to select one of the wishes; for instance, one wish might be to win one dollar every day for ten years.

- Offer discounts to people who pay with cash.

- Offer family discounts.

- Create a new product with a holiday theme.

6. Idea Diary

Ideas are fleeting creatures. Sometimes they dart by and we capture them easily; other times they are more elusive and slip away into nothingness. Now they're here, now they're not.

The mind works in mysterious ways. We often think of ideas at the darndest times—in the shower, right before we fall asleep, right after we wake up, while driving, while talking with a friend, or even when working on an unrelated problem. Trouble arises when we can't remember these ideas.

One solution to this problem is to begin an idea diary—a book or journal designed solely to record random ideas. All you have to do is get a little notebook and carry it with you. In our high-tech world, you may also want to consider a Personal Information Manager (PIM) computer, a notebook computer, or a product such as Apple Computer's Newton—a hand-held computer with a small screen that records text and other data entered with a stylus.

Regardless of the type of diary you use, the important thing is to write down ideas whenever you think of them. Also, be certain to keep your diary where you can retrieve it on demand. (If you've been writing down ideas on little slips of paper, you know how frustrating it can be to keep track of them.)

Keeping a diary handy is especially important if you ever wake up with a wonderful idea still fresh in your mind. Many famous discoveries reportedly resulted from dreams (such as atomic fission and the structure of the DNA molecule). Your ideas may not be as important, but they're yours, so treasure and capture them.

7. Mental Breakdown

Chunking, in the world of information theory, has nothing to do with peanut butter or throwing things away. It has everything to do with managing information. Basically, chunking refers to the practice of breaking information down into smaller pieces, or chunks.

We define problems, after all, by how much information we have about them. The more information we have, the more structured the problem is. And the more structured a problem is, the easier it is to solve. Thus, the better we are at managing information, the better we should be at solving problems. Unfortunately, it's not always quite that simple.

If we have trouble solving problems, we may assume we aren't creative, knowledgeable, or motivated enough. Frequently, however, the major difficulty is perceived information overload. The information itself then becomes another problem on top of the original one.

Information scientists suggest dividing information into smaller, more manageable chunks to avoid overload. Like a computer, the human mind can process only a limited number of information bits at one time (some say the mind can process an average of seven bits simultaneously). Given this limitation, it's no wonder we can't resolve large, complex problems without making some adjustments.

One way to compensate for our techno-biological deficiencies is to list subproblems (or related problem components) and work on them in order of priority. The result is a series of related, yet smaller and more manageable, problems. Frequently, attacking a problem in this manner can lead to even more creative perspectives.

Suppose, for example, your problem is deciding how to develop a new product marketing strategy. The amount of data for such a problem is immense. All sorts of demographics exist to confuse problem solvers. Rather than attempt to resolve this problem completely, it is much easier and more efficient to break it down into more manageable parts.

For instance, you could generate a list of subproblems related to various marketing tactics that form a part of the larger strategy:

- How can we better define our market niche?

- How can we better define our product mix?

- How can we better promote our products?

- How can we better move existing products to existing markets?

- How can we better move new products to existing markets?

- How can we better move new products to new markets?

- How can we improve perceived customer product values?

- How can we improve packaging designs?

The list of potential subproblems could go on and on. Although it may seem obvious to subdivide a larger problem this way, this approach may be overlooked. This is especially true when problem solvers become overwhelmed by the enormity of the task facing them.

8. Music Mania

Music hath charms to soothe the savage beast.

James Bramston
(1729)

Music has a calming effect on our emotions that can help us generate ideas. Research has shown that certain types of music can affect moods and productivity.

Our brain centers associated with emotional responses are also linked to our ability to function creatively. Music has the potential to stimulate these brain centers and help us think of creative ideas. If you think about it, both music and creativity involve similar processes and features such as intuition, abstract symbols, and holistic interpretations of data. Musical composition is a creative activity as well.

Given this relationship between music and creativity, it makes sense that music can help stimulate new ideas. There are at least three ways to use music when problem solving:

❶ Use music to help induce a relaxed mental state. Of course, you'll have to select music that helps you relax. Then get comfortable and think pleasant thoughts. Let your mind drift. Do this for at least five minutes. Next, start writing ideas, without judging them. Try to list as many as you can for another five minutes. Then relax and listen to the music at least once more before writing down ideas again.

❷ Listen to a relaxing, but lively, song all the way through. Listen to it again and focus your attention on what the music is trying to say to you. Notice any changes in mood, tempo, beat, or sound level, sudden chord changes, and so on.

Listen to the song a third time, but now concentrate on general concepts suggested by the music. For instance, a sudden change in tempo may suggest surprise, a slow portion may suggest caution, and a loud part may suggest power.

As you listen, write down these concepts. Then look over all the concepts and use them to help stimulate ideas.

❸ Use the lyrics of one or several different songs as stimulators. As you listen, write down words, phrases, or complete sentences that intrigue you. For instance, you might write down (1) "drives me wild," (2) "maybe it's the clothes she wears," (3) "you know even though the river is wide," (4) "in the middle of the night," and (5) "on the radio."

Suppose your problem involves how to motivate employees to maintain clean office areas. The lyrics you wrote down might suggest ideas such as (1) sponsoring a clean office contest and giving the winner a free rental car for the weekend, (2) holding a fun fashion contest in which participants model clothes using trash picked up in the office, (3) buying an extra-wide vacuum cleaner, (4) requiring the messiest employees to stay late to clean their offices, and (5) hiring a local disk jockey to name messy office workers on the radio and remind them that they need to be more tidy.

9. Name Change

We play name games every day. Whenever we refer to a person, object, place, or concept, we use labels known as names. The words "George," "book," "beach," and "gravity" all are names we use to communicate. Without such words, we would have trouble understanding one another. Thus, daily interactions involve a series of communication attempts using labels.

When we confront problems, we classify and identify them with labels such as "financial," "marketing," "personnel," or "quality control." These labels help us distinguish among different types of problems and provide a common basis for understanding. If I say I have a personnel problem, then you know I have a problem involving people. You may not know exactly what my problem is, but the label "personnel" helps you narrow the problem down and eliminate other types of problems as possibilities.

Although labels are essential for effective communication, they can make problem solving more difficult. One danger of labeling problems is that we may stereotype certain problems. If taken to the extreme, this tendency can restrict our ability to think of solutions.

Defining a problem with a label limits how we perceive the problem. It can create a narrow perspective even when none was intended. For instance, suppose you define a particular personnel problem as "How can we motivate employees to work harder?" Such a definition limits possible solutions for motivating employees. Although there is nothing intrinsically wrong with limiting solutions, it does decrease management's options.

In this case, it might have been better to broaden the definition with a less restrictive, more positive label. For instance, the problem might be better defined as "How can we improve employee productivity?" This switch from a motivation label to a productivity label opens up more solution alternatives and shifts the emphasis away from employees being a "problem." Thus, the situation is transformed from a motivation problem to a productivity problem.

Another approach may also help you avoid the limits imposed by problem labels. All you have to do is exercise your creativity and restate your problem. If possible, do this in a humorous way. For instance, you might restate the employee motivation problem as "how to light a fire under their tails" or "how to squeeze blood out of a stone." You could even use these perspectives to stimulate ideas. For instance, the concept of lighting a fire might suggest an employee camping trip or a weekend retreat to discuss ways to improve productivity.

10. Stereotype

This brain booster, like the Brain Borrow method [2], is based on the concept of getting a new perspective by consulting someone else. However, instead of actually talking with another person, you think as if you were someone else.

Select some occupation and think of how a stereotypical person in that position would try to resolve your problem. How would a police officer, lawyer, accountant, chemist, physician, butcher, or carpenter define your problem? What kinds of solutions would the person think of?

When you select an occupation, don't worry if you don't know much about it. What's important is that you make a concentrated effort to use whatever you know as idea stimulation. Here are the steps:

 Select an occupation you have some knowledge of and find interesting. Ideally, this occupation should be unrelated to your problem. For instance, if your problem involves healthcare, don't select a doctor or nurse.

❷ Write down everything you know (or think you know) about the occupation and the people in it. Defer all judgment when doing this.

❸ Use this list of occupational data to stimulate ideas.

Suppose, for instance, you want to improve quality control in your manufacturing process. You might select the occupation of carpenter and write the following notes about carpentry:

❢ A carpenter pounds nails on the tip with a hammer to prevent splitting wood.

❢ A good carpenter always "measures twice and cuts once."

- The quality of sanding determines the quality of the final finish.

- It's easier to saw wood with the grain than against it.

- Always use the right tool for the job (for instance, don't use a screwdriver as a hammer).

These descriptions then might prompt the following ideas:

- "Blunt" the impact of errors by developing a quality program that "hammers" on the theme of quality improvement.

- Require all manufacturing employees to check their output twice.

- Provide all employees with additional training in quality control methods.

- Conduct regular meetings with employees to make sure they are aligned with management's goals and philosophy.

- Make sure all employees use the latest technology to improve job quality.

11. Switcheroo

Switcheroo is based on the old saying "You can't see the forest for the trees." We sometimes get so close to our

BRAIN BOOSTERS FOR BUSINESS ADVANTAGE

problems that we lose the perspective needed to generate creative ideas.

One way to overcome this difficulty is to shift all your effort and thoughts to another problem. This problem should be different from the original one. Go ahead and try to resolve this second problem. Then, if you still have the time and energy, resume work on the original problem.

Switching problems in this manner will often allow you to see the original problem differently. The break from the problem provides a change in perspective. Moreover, working on the new problem often sparks ideas for the first problem. If switching to another problem doesn't help, try switching to nothing—just take a break from your problem.

12. Wake Up Call

Most of the brain boosters in this book help you generate ideas by actively engaging your brain. That is, you consciously use your brain to free associate or force together stimuli to produce something new.

There is another way to bring out ideas, however—a more passive way. It actually requires little effort on your part, and you don't have to do anything drastically different from what you do every day. All you have to do is go to sleep and then wake up. A definite no-brainer.

What is involved in this booster is harnessing the power of your brain waves. To do this requires a little knowledge about brain activity: Your brain functions at varying levels of intensity depending on the time of day. Theta waves appear during sleep, whereas beta waves are predominant when you're active during the day.

Some research has suggested that different brain wave patterns are related to different problem-solving actions. For instance, theta waves help you generate ideas, whereas beta waves are better for analytical thinking.

Theta waves are abundant just before you fall asleep and just after you wake up. Here's a little exercise to take advantage of this fact:

❶ Set your alarm clock to awaken you twenty to thirty minutes earlier than usual in the morning.

❷ Note what time it is when you wake up and quickly begin writing down ideas about some problem. As you list your ideas, suspend all judgment.

❸ Continue writing ideas until you can't think of any more. Then note what time it is.

❹ The next morning, repeat steps 1 through 3, but try to spend five more minutes writing ideas. If you run out of ideas before the five minutes is up, keep writing whatever you can think of, even if the ideas seem impractical.

❺ Continue this exercise for four or five more days.

❻ Review all the ideas and try to transform the impractical ideas into more practical ones.

CHAPTER
5

Ticklers

Tickler brain boosters will tickle, tease, and tantalize ideas out of your brain. These boosters pull out what you know exists, but couldn't think of at the time; what you thought existed, but didn't know for sure; and sometimes what you didn't even know existed. When you use ticklers, ideas will pop out surprisingly fast.

Ticklers provide the stimulus materials you need to free-associate. A tickler is anything that stimulates an idea. You probably use many brain ticklers already. For instance, have you ever tried to think of an idea and found yourself thinking of something else instead? You may be distracted temporarily by a clock on the wall. As you examine the clock, you think of things related to time. Suddenly the concept of time triggers an idea related to the problem.

As an illustration, suppose Sally is looking for creative ways to sell a product to a really tough customer. As she considers various alternatives, she happens to glance at the clock on the wall. She absentmindedly looks at the clock and immediately focuses on the concept of time. Then she begins thinking about her customer and several ideas pop out in succession:

- Call his secretary and find out at what time he is in his best mood.

- Offer him a limited-time offer.

- Give him a watch if he buys the product.

- Send him data on how the product will help him save time.

The techniques described in this chapter do essentially the same thing as the clock in this example: they stimulate ideas. However, these methods make the process a little more systematic and help target your efforts more efficiently.

Ticklers stimulate ideas using one of three general sources of stimulation:

❶ Words

❷ Pictures

❸ Objects

Examples of ticklers using words include A Likely Story [15], Excerpt Excitation [13], PICLed Brains [16], and Say What? [19]. Pictures are used with Picture Tickler [17] and Rorschach Revisionist [18]. Finally, Idea Shopping [14] is an example of a tickler using objects.

When using ticklers, defer all judgment while generating ideas. The only time you should even consider judging ideas during idea generation is when you are using multiple tickler techniques.

If you use more than one tickler, you might select the best ideas after using each technique. Then you could go on to the next method and generate ideas without judging. After you have done this for several ticklers, go back and review all your ideas. Often you'll find that the ideas you review will help stimulate even more ideas.

13. Excerpt Excitation

I quote others only the better to express myself.

Montaigne

Writers frequently use quotations to emphasize important points or to provide different perspectives on a topic. This ability to provoke new perspectives gives quotations the potential to tickle your brain and generate new ideas. As William Thackeray once said, "The two most engaging powers of an author are to make new things familiar, familiar things new."

Excerpt Excitation uses quotations to help you think of ways to make familiar things new. That's an essential ingredient of creative thinking—taking what appears to be known and applying some unique twist to it. Quotations do this by forcing you to consider angles you might otherwise have overlooked. Here are the steps for using quotations:

❶ Read a list of quotations from various authors covering different topics.

❷ Select one of the quotations and think about its meaning. Free associate if you wish and write down whatever comes to mind.

❸ Select another quotation and repeat step 2 until you have generated as many ideas as you can. (Don't be discouraged if not all quotations spark ideas. That's not the purpose of this tickler. If even one quotation triggers one good idea, then it was worth the effort.)

Several books on quotations are available in your local library or bookstore (or perhaps even your own bookshelf). You may want to select quotations that pertain to your problem topic. For instance, for the employee theft problem discussed in the previous booster, you could look for quotations about security or temptation. However, quotations from almost any area can provoke ideas.

Here are some quotations that apply to the problem of employee theft:

Security Quotations

Probe the earth and see where your main roots run.

Henry David Thoreau

The fly that doesn't want to be swatted is most secure when it lights on the fly swatter.

G. C. Lichtenberg

I believe...that security declines as security machinery expands.

E. B. White

Man's security comes from within himself, and the security of all men is founded upon the security of the individual.

Manly Hall

It's an old adage that the way to be safe is never to be secure....Each one of us requires the spur of insecurity to force us to do our best.

Harold W. Dodds

Temptation Quotations

What makes resisting temptation difficult, for many people, is that they don't want to discourage it completely.

Franklin P. Jones

All the things I really like to do are either immoral, illegal, or fattening.

Alexander Woollcott

I find I always have to write something on a steamed mirror.

Elaine Dundy

The only way to get rid of temptation is to yield to it....I can resist everything but temptation.

Oscar Wilde

Don't worry about avoiding temptation—as you grow older, it starts avoiding you.

The Old Farmer's Almanac

To illustrate how to use quotations to generate ideas, consider the employee theft problem again. The two lists of quotations helped tickle my brain and led to the following ideas:

- ♀ Install weight-sensitive pressure pads in storeroom areas that would trigger alarms when stepped on during closed times (from "Probe the earth and see where your main roots run").

- ♀ Conduct intensive background checks of all current and future employees (from "The fly that doesn't want to be swatted").

- Reward employees with free trips to dude ranches when they reduce theft (from "Each one of us requires the spur of insecurity to force us to do our best").

- Assign in-house "marshals" to monitor employee behavior (from "Each one of us requires the spur of insecurity to force us to do our best").

- Attach small, easy-to-conceal alarms on valuable items so that an alarm sounds when an item is removed from a room (from "I believe...that security declines as security machinery expands").

- Install one-way mirrors in high-risk areas (from "I find I always have to write something on a steamed mirror").

- Use items that are often stolen as performance rewards (from "The only way to get rid of temptation is to yield to it").

- Assign big brothers and sisters to new employees to help with general orientation and to educate new workers about theft (from "Don't worry about avoiding temptation—as you grow older, it starts avoiding you").

14. Idea Shopping

This tickler encourages you to do something you may not need encouragement for: put on your shoes, hop in your car, head for the nearest shopping mall, and shop until you drop! If you like to shop, you'll like this technique. With it, you can take care of two needs at once: you can buy yourself something spiffy to wear or check out all the latest goods, and you can generate some ideas as well.

Here's all you have to do: walk through a store and browse. (You know how to browse, don't you? Just put your feet together and walk.) Here are the steps:

❶ Walk around a department or discount store and take in the sights. Check out the merchandise. Watch how things are done, how people act, and so forth. Take it all in.

❷ Select one item or action that catches your eye. Examine it more closely. Notice which particular attributes, characteristics, functions, concepts, or principles are represented.

❸ Think of how this product or process might help you resolve your problem. Perhaps it can't help you directly, but you can free-associate and see what ideas the item or action might trigger. Write down any ideas that come to mind (always carry a notepad).

❹ Select something else and see what ideas it might stimulate. Continue selecting and examining stimuli until you have generated several ideas (five to ten selections usually are enough).

❺ Treat yourself and buy one of the products.

Tips

- Don't spend all your time in one department. Choose ticklers from a variety of areas.

- Stores are such rich sources of stimulation that they can be overwhelming. Don't try to take in too much. Instead, focus your attention as much as possible on things that interest you.

To illustrate Idea Shopping, suppose you are trying to reduce employee theft at your company. You've tried asking the employees not to steal, but you haven't been successful. It's time to develop more creative ideas.

You head for your local Roof-Mart. After cruising the parking lot looking for a space, you finally find a spot near the garden department entrance. You begin to browse, and you spot a garden hose. Aha!

- 🕯 *Idea:* Hide video cameras inside the overhead sprinklers. Connect the sprinklers to a water tank containing ammonia. If a security guard spots someone stealing something, the sprinklers automatically go off, spraying the thief's eyes with ammonia. (The thief will hate it when that happens.)

You continue browsing and notice that there are two rows of checkout stands, staggered in position to permit passage.

- 🕯 *Idea:* Install two sets of motion detectors, one near the entrance of a storage room and the other inside the room. The first set serves as a silent alarm to notify you someone is trying to enter; the second lets you know if the person enters the room.

You then walk down an aisle and see flashlights.

- 🕯 *Idea:* Install airport x-ray machines at all company exits.

After looking at the flashlights, you turn a corner and see an employee restocking shelves while standing on a ladder. You walk under the ladder and the employee accidentally drops a wrench on your head.

- 🔵 *Idea:* Require that employees order all supplies by computer with a user ID. Employees may pick up supplies only after the computer ID has been checked and matched to the particular supplies.

15. A Likely Story

Have you ever wanted to write the Great American Novel (GAN), but didn't think you could? Well, now's your chance. Even if you don't consider yourself a writer, you can compose a brief, fantasy story. You then you can use your story as the basis for your GAN.

Writing, like painting and sculpting, is a creative activity. All artists use a variety of stimuli to craft their creative products using free association. Some of these stimuli come from the product itself. Thus, an artist might draw a shape which stimulates another shape which prompts a third and so forth. Creative writing works much the same way. A creative phrase, character description, or plot element might suggest other corresponding thoughts which, in turn, suggest even more. In addition, creating a story about a problem forces you to consider new information and new perspectives that might have gone unnoticed before.

A Likely Story generates ideas using random stimulation from data you generate. It helps you to explore your subconscious creative thoughts and to use these thoughts to stimulate ideas. And it can be fun, too! All you have to do is write a brief fictional story, extract themes and thoughts from it, and use the extracts to spark ideas.

Remember these two points when writing your own Likely Story. First, you don't have to be a polished writer. Writing skill is not all that important for this booster. Your story is for you and you only. Moreover, too much concern with writing mechanics even may hinder your creativity. A playful attitude toward your problem is important. Let go and try to be creative. Your intuition can be your guide. Second, start with a fictional story which is unrelated to your problem. Try something whimsical or use science fiction. Humorous stories seem to work especially well. A major advantage of unrelated stories is that they maintain a fresh perspectives not possible from focusing directly on a problem.

Here are the steps:

❶ Write a brief, fictional story of less than 500 words (about two, typed, double-spaced pages). Your story should be related directly to your problem. Don't worry if your story doesn't make a lot of sense. Just let go of your imagination and see what you have lurking inside. Sometimes, humorous stories work best, but don't limit yourself.

❷ Read your story carefully. Scrutinize it for major themes, concepts, principles, actions, thoughts, and whatever else strikes your fancy. Make a list of these.

❸ Use your list as stimuli and write down any ideas suggested.

To illustrate A Likely Story, I'll use the problem of helping a publisher sell more books. Here's my story, written entirely with free association. In this case, I just write down the lead sentence and then go from there.

It was a day like any other day for Duke Smithers, private investigator. Eleanor Making wanted him to follow her husband for investigation of possible infidelity. Sleazy bars and cheap motels were what he knew best in these cases. One lead led to another like liquid molten lead. First a bartender sees the suspected couple and then a motel clerk denies ever seeing them. It was as if people knew how to disappear into thin air.

The thought of it made him gasp for air, and then parched for a drink. Yeah. A good stiff drink of cranberry juice was what he needed. He opened his desk drawer, retrieved the quart bottle of CJ (Cranberry Juice), and slammed it down on his desk. He untwisted the lid and thought of what he had learned so far: Mr. Making was making time with Susie Turnoverton, his former secretary who now worked as a CPA. Or was she? The more he reflected while sipping his CJ, the more he thought of how much he liked CJ. And then he passed out, a stream of red flowing from his mouth. Murdered or just resting? Who can tell?

O.K. It's a pretty stupid story. If it can help generate ideas, however, then it's a pretty smart story. To generate ideas for the problem of selling books, I could read over the story several times and think of ideas stimulated. (Another option would be to list major themes and write them down.) Here are some ideas:

❶ Hire an actor to play a fictional detective to promote a detective novel (from "private investigator").

❷ Start a "Frequent Purchasers" club and reward faithful customers with discounts or free books (from "infidelity").

❸ Sell popular paperbacks in hotels and motels (from "sleazy motels).

❹ Sponsor a contest with an airplane trip as the grand prize (from "disappear into thin air").

❺ Add a pine-scented scratch-and-sniff on the cover of a book about trees (from "gasp for air").

❻ Advertise health food and recipe books on bottles of fruit juice (from "cranberry juice").

❼ People receive a trade-in allowance on old books when buying new ones (from "Turn-overton").

❽ Allow people to buy books on the installment plan (from "CPA").

❾ Pass out book fliers with coupons in malls (from "passed out").

❿ Capsules ooze fake blood from inside murder-mystery books (from "red flowing from his mouth").

16. PICLed Brains

If you think about it, you've probably had your brain tickled many times while listening to someone talk. Although you may not have heard every word the person said, you selectively scanned the output and focused on a few words and phrases. These words and phrases are the ones that frequently spark new ideas.

Sometimes you may not be aware that you are influenced by someone's words; at other times, you may have an instant "aha!" when you hear a certain word. In either case, the ideas usually flow freely.

PICLed Brains is based on the Product Improvement CheckList (see Appendix) and uses a similar process to generate ideas. However, instead of relying on someone else's words, you can use random stimulus words, most of which should be unrelated to your problem.

This booster is based on the brain's ability to free-associate when presented with something new. When you first confront a new word, a stream of mental associations is triggered in your brain. Each of these mental associations has the potential to spark unique ideas, mostly because the associations are unrelated to your problem.

The Product Improvement CheckList contains stimulus words organized into four categories:

❶ Try to...(for example, inflate it, twist it, sketch it, wipe it, tighten it)

❷ Make it...(for example, transparent, soft, magnetic)

❸ Think of...(for example, time bombs, escalators, oatmeal)

❹ Take away or add...(for example, anticipation, layers, sex appeal, friction)

To generate ideas, randomly select a word from one of the four categories and see if it suggests any new ideas. You may want to free-associate from this word to get started.

To illustrate PICLed Brains, consider the problem of improving a common household flashlight. You might generate the following types of ideas:

- Make a flashlight buoyant so it floats in water if dropped accidentally (from "Try to inflate it").

- Make the flashlight handle out of rubber so it can be twisted into different shapes as a novelty or secured to some object in order to target the light beam (from "Try to twist it").

- Make the flashlight transparent, like a transparent telephone (from "Make it transparent").

- Include a timer so the flashlight turns off automatically after a certain amount of time (from "Think of time bombs").

- Design the flashlight so that it turns on whenever pressure is applied to the handle (from "Take away or add anticipation").

17. Picture Tickler

Look at the picture of the windmill in Figure 5-1. Does it suggest any images to you? Any specific associations? Thoughts? Feelings? If so, the visual stimuli in the picture have affected you. These same stimuli can also help you think of ideas— either as an individual or in a group.

Figure 5-1. Windmill

Many people respond best to visual stimuli when generating ideas. If you tend to create mental images when generating ideas, you will probably respond well to visual stimuli.

One way to test whether you are a visual thinker is to ask someone to observe your eyes while you think of a creative solution to some problem. If you look to the left and up, you are probably conjuring up visual images. (This is true because the right side of the brain—which is involved with creativity—controls the left side of the body.) Even if you are not a visual thinker, however, you can still benefit from using Picture Tickler. Here's how to use this booster:

❶ Select a variety of pictures. Color pictures from such magazines as *National Geographic* work well. The best pictures are those with a variety of actions, objects, colors, textures, and other stimuli. Try to select pictures that vary in content. For instance, you don't want to end up with all factory scenes or pictures of the countryside. In general, avoid pictures with people in them, especially closeups.

❷ Start with a picture that is unrelated to your problem. Describe the picture in detail, noting any relationships, concepts, and principles present. In particular, describe whatever action you see, actual or implied.

The purpose of this tickler is to stimulate ideas, not to achieve correctness.

Don't worry about the accuracy of your descriptions. Even if you describe something incorrectly, it doesn't matter. This reminder is especially important in groups, because members are likely to disagree with someone else's description of a picture.

❸ Look over all your descriptions and see which ones might stimulate ideas. Free-associate. If you are in a group, you may want to take turns free-associating aloud. And be playful with your associations. This way you'll be more likely to ensure fresh perspectives. Rigidity is an enemy of creative thinking.

Here's an example of how to use a picture of a windmill as a tickler. The problem involves improving a household telephone. First, describe the picture shown in Figure 5-1:

> There is a windmill. It is down by the old windmill stream (not the river, but the stream). It's where I first met you. The air is relatively calm. The wind turns the blades, which turn gears to pump water out of the fields. The faster the wind blows, the faster the blades turn. The windmill building provides protection from the elements. Many windmills are needed to pump out all the water.

Next, use the descriptions to spark ideas. Here are some examples:

❢ Put the telephone on tiny wheels to roll around on a desk (from "The wind turns the blades").

- Add an LCD panel that shows your name and welcomes you every time you pick up the phone to make a call (from "It's where I first met you").

- Make a telephone receiver that is shaped like a boat and floats in water (from "pump water out of the fields").

- Use different sound effects to notify users of incoming calls, such as driving rain, pounding surf, or hail (from "The windmill building provides protection from the elements").

- Create an inflatable telephone (from "pump out all the water").

18. Rorschach Revisionist

This brain booster uses what psychologists call "ambiguous stimulus materials." To keep things simple, we'll call them ASM. ASM are stimuli that have no apparent meaning. Instead, we tend to project meaning on these stimuli based on how we interpret the world.

A psychologist, for instance, might use Rorschach inkblots to determine if a client has an aggressive personality. The client will presumably project aggressive tendencies in response to seeing the inkblots. Another person with a different personality might describe feelings of tranquility in response to the same inkblot.

Rorschach Revisionist is based on the principle of standard inkblot tests. However, instead of using inkblots to assess your personality, you use them as sources of stimulation to generate ideas. Thus, instead of projecting your personality, you'll project your ideas and thinking perspectives.

The steps are similar to those of other tickler techniques:

❶ Create some inkblots and describe what you see in as much detail as possible. You will probably see many different images in each inkblot, so list all of them. Turn the inkblot upside down and sideways. Look at it straight down and from an angle. Squint at it, touch it, and rotate it. *Caution:* Try not to fixate on the first image you see, or you'll have trouble seeing other images.

❷ Use your descriptions as stimuli to generate ideas. However, don't restrict yourself to generating ideas directly from the stimuli. For example, if you see nothing but animals in an inkblot, don't feel you must use only animals as your stimuli. Instead, let your intuition take over. Concentrate on the inkblot and let the free associations flow. Then write down whatever ideas come to mind.

To demonstrate this tickler, we'll use the inkblot shown in Figure 5-2 to stimulate ideas for improving a telephone.

First, describe the inkblot:

I see

- A jet aircraft with swept-back wings
- Two Siamese twins on a teetertotter in the large part on the top of the inkblot
- A spider
- A frog holding a modern sculpture
- An Amazon beetle
- A moon-landing craft
- A mirror image of stalagmites
- The remains of a spider dropped from a twenty-story building
- Two alligators with Siamese twins on their backs
- A Vulcan tree root

Figure 5-2. Inkblot

Next, use the descriptions and any intuitive reactions to generate ideas:

- A children's telephone in the shape of a fighter airplane (or frog, spider, beetle, spaceship, or alligator)

- A teetertotter type of telephone in which the phone base goes down when the receiver is lifted (and vice versa)

- A telephone designed as a copy of a modern sculpture

- A telephone that "walks" across the table toward you when it rings

- A stainless steel telephone

- An alligator telephone that cradles the receiver in its mouth

- A "piggyback" telephone that contains a detachable cellular phone and a computer database of names and addresses

- A telephone that comes apart as a puzzle

19. Say What?

Idea generation should be like a rolling stone that gathers no moss. You should be able to free-associate so fast you don't have time to judge your ideas. This is especially true in groups, in which people in glass houses shouldn't throw stones: if you criticize others' ideas, you should criticize your own. Nevertheless, what is right is right. Right as rain, as a matter of fact. You should just let it go and get in the groove.

Figures of speech liven up what we read and hear. They give substance to our communications and can convey intended meanings more clearly. They can also become tiresome if used repetitively or improperly, as illustrated in the previous paragraph.

We all use clichés, proverbs, and maxims as part of our everyday speech. If you want to use them to boost your brain power, you just have to use them systematically.

A list of sixty sayings follows. Whenever you want some fresh ideas, scan over the list and see what ideas pop out. If you prefer, you can follow a more structured procedure:

❶ Review the list of sayings and select four or five that look interesting.

❷ Select one of the sayings and write down what you think is the intended meaning behind it. Use as much detail as you can.

❸ Examine your descriptions and see what ideas they suggest. Look for possible concepts, values, principles, or teachings that might apply to your problem.

Clichés, Proverbs, and Maxims

- A friend in need is a friend indeed.

- A penny saved is a penny earned.

- A rolling stone gathers no moss.

- A stitch in time saves nine.

- Absence makes the heart grow fonder.

- Actions speak louder than words.

- All roads lead to Rome.

- All that glitters is not gold.

- All work and no play makes Jack a dull boy.

- An ounce of prevention is worth a pound of cure.

- Beggars can't be choosers.

- Better late than never.

- Better safe than sorry.

- Big oaks from little acorns grow.

- Don't bite off more than you can chew.

- Don't borrow from Peter to pay Paul.

- Don't burn a candle at both ends.

- Don't put all your eggs into one basket.

- Don't rock the boat.

- Early to bed and early to rise makes a man healthy, wealthy, and wise.

- Every cloud has a silver lining.

- Experience is the best teacher.

- Familiarity breeds contempt.

- Fools rush in where angels fear to tread.

- For every drop of rain that falls, a flower grows.

- Forewarned is forearmed.

- Go ahead, make my day!

- Good fences make good neighbors.

- He who hesitates is lost.

- He who tends a fig tree will eat its fruit.

- His bark is worse than his bite.

- It never rains but it pours.

- It takes two to tango.

- It's easier to catch flies with honey than with vinegar.

- Jack of all trades, master of none.

- Keep your nose to the grindstone.

- Look before you leap.

- Loose lips sink ships.

- Misery loves company.

- Neither a borrower nor a lender be.

- Nothing ventured, nothing gained.

- Out of sight, out of mind.

- People who live in glass houses shouldn't throw stones.

- Rome wasn't built in a day.

- Seeing is believing.

- Something must be seen to be believed.

- Spare the rod and spoil the child.

- Stone walls do not a prison make.

- The early bird gets the worm.

- The grass is always greener on the other side of the fence.

- The meek shall inherit the earth.

- The pen is mightier than the sword.

- Too many cooks spoil the broth.

- Two heads are better than one.

- Two's company and three's a crowd.

- Waste not, want not.

- Where there's smoke there's fire.

- You can lead a horse to water, but you can't make him drink.

- You can't judge a book by its cover.

- You're barking up the wrong tree.

To illustrate this tickler, consider the problem of how to recruit professional employees. To generate ideas, I'll use two proverbs.

The first is "Stone walls do not a prison make." My thoughts on this proverb are listed below:

- Although you can imprison my body, you can't imprison my spirit.

- Many people create their own "mental" prisons that restrict their ability to think creatively.

- Stone walls are generally built from the bottom up in layers.

- It is much easier to go over, under, or around stone walls than through them.

These interpretations spark the following ideas:

- Emphasize personal and professional growth opportunities, or if they don't exist, create them (from "you can't imprison my spirit").

- Demonstrate in-house creativity sessions at professional meetings to show how much fun it is to work for your company and how creativity is encouraged (from "Many people create their own mental prisons").

- Provide intensive orientation sessions to lay a good foundation for understanding the company (from "Stone walls are generally built up in layers").

- Promise new executives direct access to upper management (from "Stone walls are generally built up in layers").

- Provide new executives with a personal mentor to help cut through the red tape during their first year on the job (from "It is much easier to go over, under, or around stone walls than through them").

For the second proverb, I have selected "All work and no play makes Jack a dull boy." My interpretation of this is as follows:

- We all occasionally need to relax and recharge our batteries.

- We should strive to achieve balance in the amount of work and play we do.

- Dull people can be unpleasant to be around.

These interpretations help me think of several ideas:

- Provide professionals with executive sabbaticals (from "We all occasionally need to relax and recharge our batteries").

- Require all employees to take a "play break" every day (from "We should strive to achieve balance in the amount of work and play we do").

- To keep people sharp, require job rotation (from "Dull people can be unpleasant to be around").

20. Text Tickler

Many people like to read for entertainment or to learn something new. For some people, there's nothing like curling up with a good novel or textbook (if you can describe yourself as "curling up" with a textbook). Reading helps tickle our gray matter, whether the material is Shakespeare or a clothing catalog. The more we read, the more stimulation we receive.

Sometimes, when we least expect it, a potential solution will pop out as we read. This may happen through some subconscious association or because we occasionally ponder a current problem while reading and something we read sparks an idea. Although such ideas may frequently occur by chance, we can make idea generation more predictable. That's where Text Tickler can help.

Text Tickler involves randomly selecting words from different sources and then using them to prompt ideas. It doesn't matter where you get the words, so long as you have a varied pool from which to choose. So get out your old books, catalogs, magazines, newspapers, or any source of words—dictionaries work especially well. Then follow these steps:

❶ Choose one reading source and randomly select a word or phrase.

❷ Examine the word or phrase and use it to trigger ideas.

❸ Choose another reading source and randomly select another word or phrase and use it to trigger ideas.

❹ Repeat this process several times until you have generated at least twenty ideas.

Here's an example of how to use Text Tickler: Assume you own a hotel chain and want to attract more customers. First, you need to select some random stimulus words. You are reading a newspaper while flying with several of your staff members to visit one of your hotels.

While reading movie reviews, you see the word "grumpy." This word sparks the idea of offering "Grumpy Room Service." All food orders are delivered by a grumpy delivery person as a novelty service. Or in another variation of

Grumpy Room Service, guests would be given a free meal if any staff member treats them grumpily.

You then look for another word and choose "research." This word triggers the idea of in-room computers with easy-to-access business databases for the business traveler.

Finally, you see the word "film" and think of installing picture phones in all the rooms. Now that you have thought of these hot ideas, you may take it easy for the rest of your flight and enjoy your newspaper.

21. Tickler Things

Everybody has things. They're all around us. Life would be boring without things. They make our world more interesting by providing us with varied stimuli.

We can see, touch, hear, taste, and smell things. Although specific things may give us pleasure or pain, all things stimulate us. They provide something to which we can react in a number of ways, depending on our personalities and previous experiences. The new perspectives things can give us are the basis for this brain booster cousin of PICLed Brains [16], Picture Tickler [17], and Text Tickler [20].

The difference between this booster and its cousins is that Tickler Things uses tangible objects to prompt ideas, whereas the others use word checklists, pictures, or random words. The steps for Tickler Things are as follows:

❶ Select an object unrelated to the problem. If you try this booster with a group, make sure the object is visible to all.

❷ Describe the object in some detail. Include physical characteristics as well as how people react to the object and use it. Action descriptions are important, so don't limit yourself to single-word nouns.

❸ Use the descriptions to stimulate ideas.

❹ Repeat steps 1 through 3 until you have generated at least twenty ideas or you run out of time.

Assume, as in the previous booster, that you are an executive flying to a hotel site with several staff members. You want more ideas for attracting customers. One of your managers suggests using an airplane seat as the stimulus object.

Right away, Nan (Ms. Creativity) Smith suggests recliner chairs in hotel rooms. Other staff members chime in with such ideas as stereo headsets in rooms and special beds with mattresses that can be raised and lowered.

Excited by how easy it is to think of ideas with this booster, you challenge your staff members to use an airplane as a stimulus. Nan immediately suggests theme hotel rooms such as aeronautical or outer space rooms. Even Robert (Mr. Analytical) Jones has an idea: join with an airline to offer special discounts for people who fly the airline and stay at your hotel.

CHAPTER
6

Combinations

To combine is to put together. When you put things together, you combine them in ways that may or may not be unique. It all depends on what you combine and who observes the result. That is, it's a matter of perspective.

Each combination is a stimulus that has the power to prompt any number of associations. And associations can help spark ideas. Thus, whatever you combine—whether related or unrelated to your problem—has the ability to yield creativity.

The brain boosters in this chapter rely on the principle of combination and the stimuli and associations that result. Some boosters combine things related to the problem, some combine things unrelated to the problem, and some combine related and unrelated things.

Combination boosters are a little like ticklers (see Chapter 5) in that both methods use various stimuli. The difference lies in how you respond to the stimuli. Ticklers provide direct stimulation; combinations stimulate more indirectly by joining together various elements in new ways.

22. Bi-Wordal

Take a word—any word. Now take another word and put them together. What do you get? Two words, of course! But you also get a certain meaning conveyed by those two words. Replace one of the words with another and the meaning conveyed by the combination may change dramatically. Thus, the stimulation value of any combination of words will vary depending on the words involved.

Here's an example: Suppose my organization wants to generate creative ways to increase the amount of money it donates to community service projects. My problem involves a combination of the words "increase" and "money." For most people, this particular combination would simply mean "get more money." Pretty simple. But it doesn't help me think of many ideas.

What if I now substitute a synonym for the word "increase"? I get out my handy computer thesaurus and look at several choices: advance, boost, jump, raise, hike, magnify, and snowball. Then, I experiment with different combinations of these words with the word "money." Thus, I can generate combinations such as "boost/money," "jump/money," "hike/money," and "magnify/money."

If I can substitute synonyms for one of the words, then I can also substitute for the other. In this case, my thesaurus provides such substitutes for the word "money" as cash, currency, greenbacks, dough, wampum, and income. Next, I combine the word "increase" with these words and get such combinations as "increase/greenbacks" and "increase/wampum."

All these combinations can stimulate ideas. For instance, I could have employees volunteer their time to help with automobile emergencies and solicit donations from those they help (from "boost/money"). Or I could ask artistic employees to design and sell jewelry to raise funds (from "increase/wampum"). You get the idea.

But wait. There's more. I don't have to limit myself to using the words "increase" or "money" in my combinations. I could also use any of the other synonyms on the lists. I'll start by making two lists of the words:

Increase	Money
Advance	Cash
Boost	Currency
Jump	Greenbacks
Hike	Dough
Magnify	Wampum
Snowball	Income

To generate ideas on how to increase money, I now select words randomly from each column, combine them, and use the new meaning to spark ideas. That's all there is to it. Here are some sample ideas:

- ♥ Sponsor a walk or run where participants contribute $5 for each mile they travel (from "hike/cash").

- ♥ Use payroll deductions for contributions (from "advance/income").

- ♥ Sponsor a carnival with shell games. People bet on the outcome. The proceeds go to charity (from "jump/currency").

- ♥ Give donors T-shirts with modified pictures of the denominations they contributed (from "magnify/greenbacks").

- ♥ Sell snow cones and doughnuts (from "snowball/dough").

23. Circle of Opportunity

In one respect, all creative activity is a gamble. You invest your time, effort, and creative abilities in some problem with an unknown outcome. You can't always predict the result. Sometimes your creative efforts may even make things worse. It's a crapshoot of the mind.

All gambling involves some form of randomness. Chance makes things interesting. It determines whether you win or lose. You can't control chance, but you can try to capitalize on it and use it to your advantage. You can use randomness, for example, to help prompt ideas. In particular, random combinations of problem attributes can create associations that lead to breakthrough ideas.

The Circle of Opportunity method, created by Michael Michalko (1991), is based on the random combination of problem attributes. Here's how it works:

❶ State the challenge you need to solve.

❷ Draw a circle and number it like a clock (with the numbers inside the circle).

❸ Generate a list of twelve attributes that are either related or unrelated to your problem. Related attributes would describe major problem features. For instance, an airline promotional campaign might include such attributes as people, costs, travel, and airports. Unrelated attributes are common to many problems. Examples include substance, structure, color, shape, texture, sound, and politics. Write each attribute next to one of the numbers.

❹ Throw one die to choose an attribute.

❺ Throw a pair of dice to choose the second attribute.

❻ Free-associate on each attribute individually and then on the two combined. Write down each association as you think of it.

❼ Look for connections between your associations and your problem. Think about what the associations remind you of, analogies suggested, and relationships between associations.

To illustrate Circle of Opportunity, suppose you want to improve a briefcase. First, construct a circle as shown in Figure 6-1 with twelve different attributes:

You roll a die and get the number 5 (security); you roll both dice and get the number 10 (materials) for the second attribute. You free-associate using these attributes: plastic, hidden, bulletproof vest, case-hardened steel, alarms, motion detectors, and video cameras. These free associations might help you think of such ideas as

♦ Installing hidden security pockets in a briefcase

♦ Constructing the briefcase out of bulletproof materials so it can be used as a shield

♦ Installing an alarm and motion detectors to go off whenever someone unauthorized tries to move the briefcase

You roll a die again and get the number 6 (padding) and then both dice and get the number 9

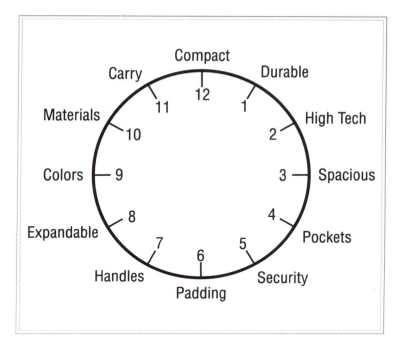

Figure 6-1. Circle of Opportunity

(colors). Your free associations are soft, spongy, pockets, and rainbow. From these associations you think of the following ideas:

- ❦ A multicolored briefcase.

- ❦ Different colors for each file of an expanding filing pocket.

- ❦ A padded handle in a contrasting color.

- ❦ A padded compartment in a contrasting color for use when carrying a notebook computer. You can remove the compartment when you aren't carrying the computer and save space.

24. Combo Chatter

This brain booster was originally known as Semantic Intuition when researchers at the Battelle Institute developed it in the 1970s (Schaude, 1979). That's certainly an impressive name, but it's a little pretentious for this book. I decided to simplify things and call it Combo Chatter.

The typical new-product process involves generating ideas, selecting the best ones, developing them into workable products, and then assigning them names. Combo Chatter reverses that process somewhat: instead of generating ideas and then names, it generates names and then ideas. Here are the steps:

❶ Generate two lists of words related to your problem. For instance, if your problem is to design a new coffee cup, you might list "things involving coffee cups" and "things involving people who drink coffee."

❷ Randomly select one word from each list and use the combination to stimulate ideas. Here's an example:

Coffee Cups	People
Handles	Tense
Hot	Addicted
Logos	Cream and sugar
Breakable	Grind beans
Spills	Carry cups

After examining different combinations, you might generate the following types of ideas:

- Squeezable handles to relieve tension (from "handles/tense")

- Squeezable handles that inject cream or sugar (from "handles/cream and sugar")

- A combination coffee cup and bean grinder (from "handles/grind beans")

- Insulated coffee cups (from "hot/carry cups")

- Cups that break down into small pieces for easy carrying (from "breakable/carry cups")

This is a nifty brain booster for at least two reasons: (1) it has the potential to create many different perspectives, and (2) it combines elements of both related and unrelated stimuli. That is, it uses attributes related directly to the problem and combines these attributes to create a more or less unrelated stimulus. Thus, it helps create perspective changes not possible with methods that rely on a single stimulus.

25. Ideas in a Box

Ideas in a Box—originally known as Morphological Analysis, or Matrix

Analysis—was developed by Zwicky (1969) to help generate scientific ideas. As with other combination methods, Ideas in a Box prompts ideas by forcing together problem attributes that lead to new ideas. Although the method has variations, the one presented here is typical. The steps are as follows:

❶ List major problem attributes across the top of a sheet of paper.

❷ List potential or existing subattributes for each category.

❸ Combine one or more subattributes from each category and use the combination to suggest ideas.

❹ Select another combination of subattributes and use it to generate ideas.

❺ Continue this process until you have generated all possible ideas.

An example will make the process clearer. Suppose you are director of packaging design for Snafu Snack Food Company. Sales of your Cheesy Chunk Crackers have been slipping. Market research indicates supermarket consumers consider two criteria when buying cheese cracker products: (1) ability of the package to catch their eyes, and (2) value-added or unique features.

You have been directed to redesign the current box to emphasize value-added features. Your boss gives you free rein to make changes.

You've just finished reading *Brain Boosters* and decide to use Ideas in a Box to help spark ideas. You set up a matrix as shown in Table 6-1:

Table 6-1.
Ideas in a Box Matrix

Container Shapes	Container Materials
Cylindrical	Cardboard
Spherical	Plastic
Rectangular	Metal
Pyramidal	Combinations

Types of Closures	Lining Materials
Ziploc®	Wax paper
Clips	Aluminum foil
Adhesive	Regular paper
Screw cap	Cellophane

Next, select one subattribute from each column. For instance, you might design a cylindrical package made of plastic with a screw top and an aluminum foil lining. Or you might select a spherical container made of combinations of materials with clips for closures and a cellophane lining. You get the idea. Although Ideas in a Box may not always prompt unique ideas, it will help you search systematically for possible combinations.

26. Ideatoons

If you liked Ideas in a Box and are a visual thinker, then you'll like Ideatoons. Ideatoons are based on the work of architects Alexander, Ishikawa, and Silverstein, who used a visual thinking method known as "pattern language" to help create new building designs.

The architects developed abstract visual symbols that substituted for words. Each symbol represented a particular problem attribute. The symbols helped bring out potential relationships between attributes that, when identified, could trigger ideas. For instance, vertical arrows might point toward a curved line at the top of a page. This symbol might then suggest different ways of supporting or building an arch.

Michael Michalko (1991) adopted this visual approach and used it to describe Ideatoons—graphic problem representations. (This technique is also similar to the Symbolic Representation method developed by VanGundy, 1983.) You don't need to be an artist to use Ideatoons—you just need the ability to draw anything remotely resembling something else. The steps involved are as follows:

❶ Divide your problem into major attributes.

❷ Illustrate each problem attribute with an abstract, graphic symbol. Put each symbol on a separate index card or small sheet of paper. Don't struggle to capture the perfect symbol. Just draw whatever seems appropriate.

❸ Place the completed cards, face up, on a table. Experiment with different groups of symbols. Don't consciously force any particular pattern.

❹ As you arrange and rearrange the symbols, use the combinations to free-associate and see what ideas are suggested. Or, just use the individual symbols to prompt ideas.

❺ If you start to run out of ideas, add another Ideatoon or begin a new set.

Suppose you are a packaging design director concerned with developing new cheese cracker box designs. First, you develop a list of problem attributes: box, package opening, closure, and package lining. Next, illustrate these attributes using graphic symbols such as the ones shown in Figure 6-2. Then, experiment with different combinations of symbols to help kick start your imagination.

Here are some sample ideas:

❦ A box with two chambers: one for crackers and one for cheese spread (from the box and package opening symbols).

❦ A box with disposable, tear-off closures. Use each closure strip only once (from the box and closure symbols).

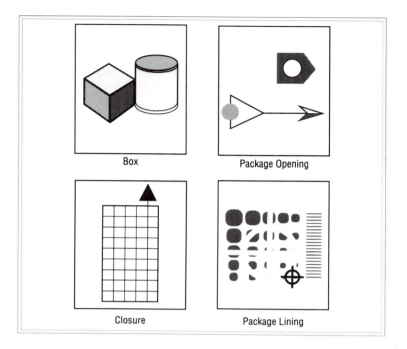

Figure 6-2. Ideatoons

- Nested package linings with a vacuum in between (from the package opening and package lining symbols).

- Put a cheese cutter inside each package so consumers can stamp out pieces of cheese to conform to the shape of different crackers (from the package opening and closure).

27. Mad Scientist

This booster, developed by Doug Hall (1994), is somewhat similar to Circle of Opportunity [23].

Instead of using a circle, however, Mad Scientist uses Green Die and Red Die lists of problem attributes. Attribute lists for each die are numbered 1 through 6.

The attributes for Mad Scientist differ from those used for Circle of Opportunity in two ways: (1) Mad Scientist categories are more general, and (2) some of the categories may be completely unrelated to the problem. The procedure for combining attributes also is different: Circle of Opportunity combines two different attributes from the circle, whereas Mad Scientist combines two different *lists* of attributes. The specific steps are as follows:

❶ List six general categories across a sheet of paper for the Green Die categories. Four or five categories should be related directly to the problem. The others may be unrelated or even somewhat whimsical. For each general category, list below it four or five examples. Thus, the briefcase materials would include leather, plastic, diamond, and metal.

❷ Do the same thing for the Red Die categories as shown in Table 6-2. (As you can see from the table, it's O.K. to use some of the same categories as in the Green Die list.)

❸ Roll a green die (or designate a white die as "green") and select a category based on the number shown.

❹ Roll a red die (or designate a white die as "red") and select a category based on the number shown.

❺ Look over the lists from both categories and generate ideas by combining one word from each category (or using any of the single words as stimuli).

To illustrate Mad Scientist, the Green and Red Die lists for the problem of improving a briefcase might be set up as shown in Table 6-2.

Let's say you roll the green die and get a 4 (Weird) and roll the red die and get a 1 (Storage). You may then use the words in these categories as stimuli by examining single words or combining different words from the two categories. Here are some sample ideas from these two categories:

♦ An Elvis briefcase shaped like a guitar with a picture of the "King" on the side (from "Elvis")

♦ A compartment with a cold pack to keep food from spoiling (from "pickles" and "pockets")

♦ Folding legs to turn a briefcase into a display case (from "frogs")

♦ A briefcase with a built-in, battery-powered compact disc player (from "Madonna" and "boxes")

Table 6-2
Example of the Mad Scientist Brain Booster

Green Die					
1	2	3	4	5	6
Places	**Materials**	**Shape**	**Weird**	**Function**	**Flavors**
Boardroom	Leather	Round	Elvis	Sprinkling	Cherry
Home	Plastic	Square	Pickles	Weight	Lemon
Office	Diamond	Sphere	Frogs	Sorting	Strawberry
Kitchen	Metal	Flat	Madonna	Flying	Chocolate
Red Die					
Storage	**Time**	**Closures**	**Weird**	**Function**	**Sizes**
Pockets	Morning	Zippers	Superman	Reminders	Executive
Boxes	Afternoon	Button	Crystal	Wake Up	Compact
Shelves	Tea	Snaps	Ears	Typing	Overnight
Files	Noon	Straps	Birthday	Faxing	Regular

A major advantage of Mad Scientist is that it provides a greater number of stimuli than the Circle of Opportunity. Although Mad Scientist takes more time to set up, the resulting stimuli are well worth the trouble.

28. Noun Action

Words, like people, can assume many different faces. Depending on our moods, we can communicate a variety of feelings and behaviors. Yet no matter how many faces we show or how many emotions we express, we still are the same person.

In a similar way, the same basic word can communicate different meanings depending on how it is used and in what form. Nouns can become verbs and vice versa. It all depends on how you use them.

You can take advantage of this versatility of words to help generate ideas. Specifically, you can experiment with different noun and verb relationships and see what ideas emerge.

For instance, consider a problem of improving a telephone. In this case, the problem involves the verb "improve" and the noun "telephone." If you switch the noun and verb you get "telephoning improvements." This combination might suggest the idea of a telephone that repairs itself automatically or a special toll-free number so customers can call the manufacturer with improvement ideas.

29. Noun Hounds

Bloodhounds are used to track people and animals. They search for a scent, lock onto it, and then pursue their quarry relentlessly. Hounds go from one scent to the next until they achieve their objective.

The Noun Hounds brain booster works in a similar manner. You start with a random noun and then go from one association to the next until you generate a sufficient number of ideas.

Noun Hounds (also called Modifier Noun Associations) was originally developed by Van-Gundy (1983, 1988) to generate new product ideas using a random noun and a modifier unrelated to the problem. You then free-associate from this combination to generate ideas. Here's how this method works:

❶ Think of a noun (person, place, thing, quality, or action) and a word that modifies it. Include some contradictory or just plain silly combinations. Some examples: flying geese, glowing apples, silent springs, intelligent shrimp, falling stars, rising elephants, quivering rocks.

❷ Select one of the noun-modifier combinations and free-associate. Write down whatever comes to mind, with each idea leading to the next.

❸ Use the noun-modifier combinations and all the associations as stimuli to generate ideas.

❹ Repeat steps 2 and 3 until you have generated enough ideas.

An example will help clarify this procedure. Suppose your objective is to improve a flashlight. You think of the combination "rising elephants." Next you free-associate: leaping trunks, swiveling suitcases, twisting airplanes, flapping wings. This process suggests the following ideas:

- A telescopic flashlight capable of holding a variable number of batteries (from "rising elephants")

- A storage compartment for small objects such as a spare bulb (from "leaping trunks")

- A hovercraft flashlight that floats above the ground or water (from "twisting airplanes")

- A flashlight with shutters for signaling (from "flapping wings")

30. Parts Is Parts

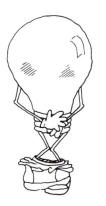

Sometimes creativity is a hit-or-miss proposition. Random stimuli may or may not spark ideas. Free associations are relatively unpredictable. You really don't know how you'll respond to a particular stimulus until you encounter it. Then, once you respond, you don't know if the resulting ideas will be winners.

There's nothing necessarily wrong with this. Unpredictability keeps things interesting and makes the occasional hot idea all the more exciting. There are times, however, when you might want to generate ideas a little more systematically. That's where Parts Is Parts may help.

Parts Is Parts is based on the "Heuristic Ideation Technique (HIT)" developed by Edward Tauber (1972). It generates ideas by creating heuristics or rules of thumb. (A rule of thumb is a guideline which increases the chances of achieving a certain outcome.) Heuristics then are used to structure the idea generation process.

Tauber believes that heuristics can make idea generation more efficient and insure that only the best idea candidates will be considered. Although HIT originally was intended for new product idea generation, it also will work for a variety of other problems.

Two heuristics help make idea generation more efficient. The first assumes that most ideas can be described using a two-word combination. For instance, the words "toaster/tart" represent a combination which might suggest a breakfast food product. The second heuristic is that some combinations will be viewed as more interesting than others. In particular, combinations that come from different categories have a greater chance of suggesting unique ideas than combinations from similar categories. As an example, the combination "ice cream/cereal" might be perceived as more interesting than the combination "vegetables/fruits."

The basic steps for Parts Is Parts are

❶ Create an idea generation grid containing attributes from two product areas. An example would be a grid which contains packaging formats (e.g., bag, boil-in-bag, box, pan, jar, can, tube) and different food forms (e.g., cookie, biscuit, gravy, bread, dressing, steak, juice, dips).

❷ Assign numbers to each possible combination (e.g. bag/dip = 1; box/steak = 2; bag/juice = 3; tube/gravy = 4).

❸ Examine all the combinations and eliminate any already on the market.

❹ Circle combinations that have the greatest potential.

❺ Create brief statements for each of the remaining combinations. Include reasons why they are interesting, why they have market potential, and how they might be used.

❻ Select the best combinations and transform them into marketable ideas.

An example of the "HIT" technique is shown below using packing formats and food forms as the two product areas or elements. A number between 1 and 24 represents each possible combination.

Combinations 7, 9, and 21 are crossed out since they represent existing products (bread in a bag, cookies in a bag, and cookies in a box). Combinations 4, 10, 11, 15, 18, and 20, however, are circled since they represent potential new product ideas. For instance the following ideas are suggested by these combinations:

❶ A dip in an aerosol spray which can be sprayed on bread or crackers (#4).

❷ Vegetable dip in a designer bag for individual dipping (#10).

❸ Different juices in a bag that can be drunk by squeezing, pouring, or using a straw (#11).

❹ Cookies in a tube—similar to potato chips in a cardboard cylinder (#15).

❺ Gravy in a tube, especially for children who can use it to write letters and draw pictures on their food (#18).

❻ Box steak lunches which can be reheated in microwavable packages (#20).

Food Forms	Packaging Formats			
	Aerosol	Bag	Tube	Box
Bread	1	✗	13	19
Steak	2	8	14	⑳
Cookie	3	✗	⑮	✗
Dip	④	⑩	16	22
Juice	5	⑪	17	23
Gravy	6	12	⑱	24

31. Parts Purge

If you like to free-associate, you'll like the Parts Purge brain booster. It was originally developed by VanGundy (1992) as Attribute Association Chains. You can use this method to generate ideas by listing problem attributes, free-associating from each attribute, and then using the free associations as stimuli for ideas. It's as simple as that: free-associate on problem parts and generate, generate, generate. Here are the specific steps:

❶ List major problem attributes.

❷ List subattributes for each major attribute.

❸ Select one of the subattributes and write down the first word you think of (that is, free-associate).

❹ Write down a second word stimulated by the first. Continue to free-associate until you have listed four or five words for each subattribute.

❺ Repeat steps 3 and 4.

❻ Use the free associations to stimulate ideas.

Suppose you want to improve a table lamp. First, list major attributes and subattributes:

♀ *Name:* table lamp

♀ *Parts:* base, bulb, cord, shade, switch

- *Shapes:* round, cylindrical, pleated
- *Functions:* illuminates, heats, collects dust
- *Material:* cloth, metal, rubber

Next, free-associate using one or more of the attributes. For example:

- *Table lamp:* lantern, cow, tipsy, shed, fire, Chicago
- *Base:* acid, soda, water, bottle, drink
- *Switch:* spank, paddle, ping pong, table, games
- *Illuminates:* lights, sky, stars, rockets, gravity
- *Metal:* heavy, light, air, breath, oxygen

Finally, use these free associations to generate ideas to improve a table lamp:

- A lampshade with shutters to create different lighting effects (from "lantern")
- A lamp with a swivel base to allow reading light adjustments (from "tipsy")
- Lampshades with panoramic pictures of major cities (from "Chicago")
- A lamp with video games built in (from "games")

- A magnetically levitated lamp (from "gravity")

- A hovercraft lamp that can be moved easily around a large table (from "air")

32. Preppy Thoughts

The boosters in this chapter generate ideas by combining related or unrelated problem attributes. Although such combinations have great potential, it sometimes helps to introduce additional stimuli.

Preppy Thoughts will help provide this variety by introducing action words into combinations. The basic procedure was originally suggested by Crovitz (1970) using a technique known as Relational Algorithms. The Preppy Thoughts method provides the same stimulation using random selections of relational words (prepositions, conjunctions, and so on). Crovitz suggested forty-two of these words:

about	at	for	of	round	to
across	because	from	off	still	under
after	before	if	on	so	up
against	between	in	opposite	then	when
among	but	near	or	though	where
and	by	not	out	through	while
as	down	now	over	till	with

VanGundy (1988) later added nineteen more:

above	behind	beyond	past	upon
along	below	during	since	within
amid	beneath	except	throughout	without
around	beside	into	toward	

To generate ideas with Preppy Thoughts, follow these steps:

❶ State the problem using an action verb and object.

❷ Select a relational word and insert it between the verb and the object.

❸ Use the new combination as an idea stimulus.

As an example, consider a problem of how a restaurant could attract more customers. The action verb and object are "attract" and "customers." Here are some possible ideas from inserting relational words between these two words:

❢ Have special community nights in which people are seated across from someone new in order to make new friends (from "attract/across/customers").

❢ Offer special low rates for meals eaten before a certain time (from "attract/before/customers").

- Place advertising fliers on cars of supermarket customers and offer them a discount in exchange for their grocery receipts (from "attract/near/customers").

- Hire a public relations firm (from "attract/about/customers").

- Add an outdoor patio (from "attract/out/customers").

- Give discounts to overweight people (from "attract/round/customers").

- Have a special room for people who like to eat on the floor (from "attract/under/customers").

- Give discounts to customers who help recruit new customers (from "attract/with/customers").

- Start an eating club with one free meal for every ten purchased (from "attract/since/customers").

- Specialize in healthy foods and offer free diet planning (from "attract/within/customers").

33. SAMM I Am

With apologies to Dr. Seuss, SAMM I Am actually refers to a method known as Sequence-Attribute Modifications Matrix. It was developed by Brooks and later described by Souder and Ziegler

(1977). SAMM I Am differs from other brain boosters in that it was designed specifically for problems involving a sequence of steps (for example, various processes). Thus, it will not be useful for more general idea generation problems. Here are the steps:

❶ List the major process activities.

❷ List basic ways to modify any process (for example, speed up, eliminate, rearrange).

❸ Construct a matrix with process steps listed on the left and potential modifications listed along the top.

❹ Examine each cell (the intersection of steps and modifications) and use it to suggest possible modifications for that step.

To illustrate SAMM I Am, suppose you want to improve the way restaurant customers pay their bills. Major activities and possible modifications are shown in Figure 6-3.

After examining the matrix, you might come up with the following ideas:

❢ Install electronic credit card machines at each table (much like those at many automobile service stations.)

❢ Eliminate paper meal checks. Allow regular customers to run a tab.

❢ Eliminate credit card papers. Handle credit card purchases electronically for

customers with electronic digital assistant pads (DAPs). Customers link up their DAPs with those of the restaurant. The transaction is then handled electronically: the customer's bank account is debited and the restaurant's account is instantly credited.

Process Activities	Potential Modifications					
	Eliminate	Substitute	Rearrange	Combine	Increase	Decrease
1. Hand bill to cashier						
2. Get out credit card						
3. Hand card to cashier						
4. Cashier processes card						
5. Cashier returns card						
6. Sign card receipt						
7. Hand receipt to cashier						
8. Cashier returns copy						

Figure 6-3. SAMM I Am

💡 Give preferred customers special credit cards that look like brass plates. When customers are ready to pay their bills, they use the brass plates (restaurant credit cards).

34. 666

Time to gamble again! Get out those dice and help Papa get a new pair of shoes (or something like that). But don't expect to win money like the devil. In fact, don't even think of the devil. The 666 brain booster has nothing to do with old Beelzebub.

The 666 method is the creation of Doug Hall (1994). It is based on principles of combination and free association and is somewhat similar to Circle of Opportunity [23] and Mad Scientist [27]. The problem elements used, however, are not organized into logical categories. As in Mad Scientist, you use dice to select elements to combine. The steps are as follows:

❶ Generate three lists of six problem elements. Number each element within each list. The elements may or may not be related to your particular problem.

❷ Label the lists "White Die," "Green Die," and "Red Die."

❸ Roll each die and select the element indicated for each list. (If you are in a group, group members may take turns rolling the dice.)

❹ Use the combination of the three elements to spark ideas.

An example using the problem of inventing new types of soup is shown in Table 6-3.

Table 6-3.
Example of the 666 Brain Booster

White Die	Green Die	Red Die
1. Cracker Jack stuff	1. Lunch time	1. Metal cylinders
2. Secret ingredients	2. Award winning	2. Exotic nutrition
3. Astronaut parties	3. Liquid delight	3. Healthy and wealthy
4. Annual physicals	4. Children's party	4. Heated flavor
5. Security time	5. Loose goose	5. Just like Mom's
6. Syrups	6. Free radical	6. Bowl full of joy

After you have rolled the dice, you may think of the following ideas:

- Gourmet soup with secret ingredients (2-3-3)

- Soup to eat after exercising (like Gatorade) (4-5-3)

- Soup cans with pictures of famous mothers (5-1-5)

- A chicken soup can with a Sterno container built into the bottom (6-5-4)

- Soup cans with prizes inside (1-6-4)

35. Word Diamond

Hot new ideas shine and sparkle with radiant brilliance. They illuminate their surroundings and

blind lesser ideas. Everyone wants a shiny, mul-tifaceted new idea, but you can't always get what you want. Sometimes you have to settle for a so-so idea.

The Word Diamond brain booster won't en-sure that all your ideas will sparkle. It will, how-ever, provide you with another systematic approach to idea generation. And it's a breeze to implement.

This technique was originally developed by VanGundy (1983) as a simple combination pro-cedure using elements of a problem statement. Thus, it is similar to Bi-Wordal [22]. Instead of using alternative word meanings, however, Word Diamond generates ideas by combining words in the problem statement in different ways. The steps are as follows:

❶ State the problem so that it contains at least four major problem attributes or elements, including both nouns and verbs.

❷ Select four major words or phrases.

❸ Arrange the words or phrases in the shape of a diamond. There should be one word at each vertex (point) of the diamond.

❹ Select one of the words or phrases, com-bine it with another, and write down any ideas prompted.

❺ Continue selecting and combining words until you have tried generating ideas from all possible combinations.

Suppose you are losing scientists to your competitors. In particular, you want to encourage more professional employees to remain in the research and development (R&D) department. First, select four words or phrases: encourage, employees, remain, and R&D. Next, arrange them in the shape of a diamond as shown in Figure 6-4:

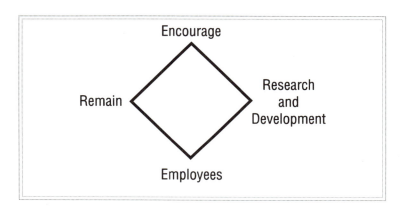

Figure 6-4. Word Diamond

Finally, use various combinations to suggest ideas:

- Give incentive rewards for employees who achieve special professional recognition (from "employees/encourage").

- Match up younger employees who are more likely to leave with older employees and form a buddy program (from "employees/encourage").

- Establish two career tracks—one managerial and one nonmanagerial—to take into account different professional growth needs (from "employees/remain").

- Develop a "Pride in R&D" public relations campaign to promote team spirit (from "R&D/employees").

CHAPTER
7

Blue Skies

Blue skies: Happy days are here again. Put on a happy face. It's time to let loose and see what happens. Be footloose and fancy-free. Go on and let go. Allow the ideas to flow and grow. Build on them. Create highways to the skies and then float back down. Light as a feather...in your cap. Tip the waiter and smile, smile, smile, all the while thinking of what might be. Set your mind free and free-associate.

Everything you read in the previous paragraph is based on free association. I started with the words "blue skies" and let loose. I had no idea where my thoughts would take me. I tried to think in the general area of idea generation, but I avoided any preconceived thoughts.

The paragraph may not be logical, but it is creative, and it contains many stimuli. That's the idea. I was able to create many thoughts and perspectives from the initial stimulus of "blue skies." Each sentence in the paragraph has the potential to stimulate additional thoughts. Even the most cliché-ridden sentence has that potential.

Stimuli trigger associations, which trigger ideas. That's how the human mind works. We flit from one concept to another.

Think about it. It's not that difficult. You can think of anything you want. That's a lot of power packed into one convoluted mass of gray matter. And it's yours. All you have to do is harness it.

Although it may seem paradoxical, the best way to harness your creative brainpower is to let go. Allow one thought to lead to another. Be playful. Forget all the analytical stuff. Take the time to sink into a "deep think."

The brain boosters in this chapter are based on the Blue Skies principle of free association. These techniques rely on your ability to let go and generate one idea or concept from another—to flit about in your mind. Each booster helps structure this process a little differently. As a result, each booster has the potential to create many different perspectives and types of ideas.

However, it's up to you to make the boosters work. The more you let go, the more you will boost your brainpower. And the more you boost your brainpower, the more ideas you'll produce.

Before you try your first Blue Skies booster, think a little about how you generate ideas. Try to get into the appropriate mind-set and think about how easy it is to flow from one thought to the next. Then, just let your mind go.

36. Brain Mapping

Make an outline for how to make a ham sandwich. Go ahead and try it. Finished? O.K. Your outline may look something like this:

I.   Get out ham.

II. Get knife.

    A. Hold ham securely.

    B. Slice ham.

III. Open package of bread.

    A. Remove two pieces.

    B. Put bread on plate.

IV. Place slice of ham on one piece of bread.

V.   Get out mustard.

    A. Open jar.

    B. Get knife.

    C. Stick knife in jar.

VI. Spread mustard on second piece of bread.

VII. Place second piece on top of ham slice.

VIII. Cut sandwich in two.

IX. Eat sandwich.

Now think through your experience. You probably spent a. lot of time thinking about the order of each activity. For instance, you may have started with "Open a package of bread" and then remembered you would need a ham. What to put next probably occupied most of your time and effort. Thus, outlines often force us to spend more time thinking about sequence than about content. They also disrupt our thinking because we have to alternate focusing on sequence and content.

Outlines are based on a "left brain" process. To improve this situation, you need a "right brain" process. You have two brain hemispheres: a logical, sequential, analytical left brain and an intuitive, holistic, creative right brain. Every time you solve a problem you use both sides of your brain. Sometimes you use the left a little more and sometimes the right.

Tony Buzan (1976) developed Brain Mapping to capitalize on the strengths of the right brain. He originally conceived of this technique as a tool to help students take notes. He soon found, however, that Brain Mapping was useful for a variety of activities including idea generation. Mind Mapping has also been popularized by Joyce Wycoff (1991).

Here are the basic steps for this technique:

❶ List all major problem elements. Include relevant people, processes, issues, time schedules, expectations, outcomes— anything that helps you understand the situation.

❷ Select the most central element and write it down on the center of a sheet of paper. This element should capture your primary concern.

❸ Draw a box or other more appropriate shape around this concern. For instance, if your concern is employee tardiness, you might draw a clock around the problem statement.

❹ Draw a line extending from one side of your central shape. Write a related word on the line.

❺ Depending on what you think of next, (a) draw another line extending from the central shape, or (b) draw a line related to a subtopic (or subattribute) for the first line.

❻ Continue drawing lines and adding topics until you have run out of ideas.

If you've never seen a brain map before, these steps may not be clear. For an example, see Figure 7-1, which shows a brain map on ways to improve a bed.

As you examine this brain map, don't expect to find all the elements placed in a logical way. For instance, I placed the ideas for awakening or helping you sleep under the "sleeping" category because that's where I thought of them. It would have made more sense to put them under the "mattress" category. But remember, it doesn't really matter how you generate ideas, just so you get them out.

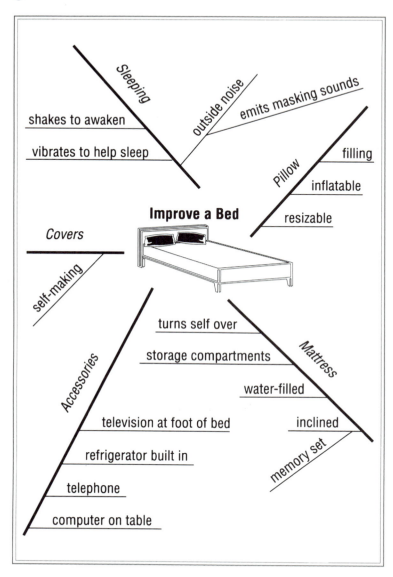

Figure 7-1. Brain Map

37. Doodles

You've probably heard the expression "That's usin' the ol' noodle!" It means, of course, that you were able to apply your brainpower effectively. Well, noodle power can also help you generate ideas with doodles.

You know how to doodle, don't you? Just start scribbling on a sheet of paper and express your creative urges. Let your pen or pencil take off and draw swirls, loops, circles, boxes, arrows, spirals, or whatever feels right. You may already have practice doodling. Most of us doodle while talking on the phone or listening to a boring speech. (Did you ever notice that there seems to be a direct correlation between how boring a speech is and how elaborate your doodles are?)

Because doodles provide an outlet for creative expression, they can also help generate ideas. VanGundy (1988) designed a technique known as Symbolic Representations, which uses doodles as the basic idea generation mechanism. Although this method is similar to Ideatoons [26], there is one major difference: the doodles are based on one or more major principles underlying the problem. This focus helps target your doodles a little more than mere random scribblings. Here are the steps:

❶ Think of the major principle underlying your problem.

❷ Draw an abstract symbol that represents this principle. Don't worry if you're not an artist. Just draw whatever pops into your mind regarding the principle.

❸ Free-associate from this symbol and draw another. Try to elaborate and provide some detail for each drawing.

❹ Continue to free-associate from each symbol and draw at least three additional ones.

❺ Examine all the symbols and use them as stimuli to generate ideas.

For example: Suppose your problem is how to attract more customers to your restaurant. The major underlying principle is attraction, or how to increase or get more of something. Draw a symbol representing this principle. Next, draw another symbol and then another until you have four or five. Sample symbols are shown in Figure 7-2.

After you have examined each doodle, the following ideas might come to mind:

🍴 Have "Dinner With a Local Celebrity" nights. After customers are seated in the restaurant between certain hours, a lottery is held and the winner gets to have dinner with a local celebrity.

🍴 Ask customers to brainstorm ideas to increase business. Give free dinners to those who suggest the best ideas.

🍴 Offer special "sampler" meals in malls.

Figure 7-2. Doodles

- Install small video monitors on tables so customers can watch their food being prepared in the kitchen.

- Offer evening river cruises with appetizers at the restaurant, the entrée on the boat, and dessert back at the restaurant.

38. Essence of the Problem

An essence is something concentrated that retains its basic properties. It is the internal factor that gives something special characteristics. For instance, perfume is the essence of flowers, and grapes are the essence of wine. Thus, an essence is a root or source element.

Because essence is a source element, it defines what is and what can be. Essence provides potential and boundaries and scope. It communicates meaning, which leads to understanding.

Each problem has an essence that defines what is and what can be. By examining the "what is," it is possible to explore the "what can be." That is, understanding essence makes it possible to extract potential ideas from problem statements, because all problems exist on a continuum of abstraction.

Some problems are relatively concrete and structured. For instance, increasing the number of parking spaces in a downtown area is relatively straightforward. On the other hand, a problem of increasing space is more abstract and much less structured. One reason is that what is increased (space) is ambiguous. The concept of increasing is known, but not in relation to space. In this case, "space" is not specified. There is no context.

Problem essence typically is abstract and lacking in definable structure. It specifies the basic aspects of a problem. Thus, the essence of the problem of increasing the number of parking spaces might be the concept of acquisition.

This booster originally was developed by William Gordon (1961) has been described by Van-Gundy (1988) as the "Gordon/Little Method." You can use the essence of a problem to help stimulate ideas by following these steps:

❶ Write out a statement of your problem.

❷ Temporarily forget this problem and think of its essence (that is, state the problem as abstractly as possible.)

❸ List ideas for resolving this abstract problem.

❹ State the problem in a slightly less abstract form.

❺ List ideas for resolving this problem.

❻ State the problem in an even less abstract form.

❼ List ideas for resolving this problem.

❽ Examine all the ideas and use them as stimuli to resolve the original problem.

To illustrate this booster, consider the problem of preventing vandalism in factory lunchrooms. The essence of this problem is the concept of prevention. Pretty simple. I temporarily forget the original problem and generate ideas to prevent things from happening:

- Tie them down.
- Bribe them.
- Glue them together.
- Shoot them.
- Hypnotize them.
- Spread rumors.

Next, I state the problem less abstractly as ways to prevent things from being broken. Ideas for this definition include the following:

- Cushion them.
- Suspend them.
- Pad them.
- Hide them.
- Strengthen them.

Finally, I state the problem even less abstractly as ways to prevent destruction of property. My ideas for this problem include the following:

- Hire security guards.

- Make it more durable.

- Store it in a secure area.

- Fine people for destruction.

- Put a fence around it.

Finally, I use all the ideas as stimuli for ideas to prevent vandalism in factory lunchrooms. Here are some possible ideas:

- Bolt down all appliances and equipment (from "tie them down").

- Provide rewards to employees who report instances of theft and vandalism (from "bribe them").

- Install video cameras in high-vandalism areas (from "shoot them").

- Require all employees to attend training sessions on problems caused by vandal-ism (from "spread rumors").

- Put pads on vending machines to prevent damage (from "pad them").

   Hire security guards to work undercover (from "hire security guards" and "hide them").

- Make equipment portable whenever possible and store it when it isn't in use (from "store it in a secure area").

● Eliminate company lunchrooms and require employees to eat outside the factory (from "put a fence around it").

39. Exaggerate That

Have you ever stretched the truth? Come on, now—be truthful. Most people have exaggerated something sometime in their life, even if it's only a slight distortion. Exaggerations not only can make us feel better, but they also can add excitement to our interactions. The more extreme and vivid our exaggerations, the more attention they will attract.

Each instance of truth stretching is a stimulus. And you know how stimuli can help generate ideas. There must be the makings of a brain booster here somewhere!

And there is. It's known as Exaggerated Objectives (Olson 1980). You generate ideas by listing problem criteria, exaggerating them in any way possible, and then using the exaggerations as stimuli to prompt ideas. The specific steps are as follows:

❶ List the major criteria (objectives) you would use to evaluate potential solutions to a specific problem.

❷ Exaggerate or stretch each criterion in any way possible. Don't be concerned with how "correct" your exaggerations are. There is no such thing as correct with this booster.

❸ Use each exaggeration as a stimulus to spark new ideas.

Suppose, for example, you want to attract more international airline passengers. You might use the setup shown in Table 7-1.

Table 7-1.
Example of Exaggerate That

Original Criteria	Exaggerated Criteria	Possible Solutions
1. Minimal cost.	1. Costs more than $1 million.	1. Have a lottery for free tickets.
2. Safety not compromised.	2. Kills thousands of passengers.	2. Offer on-board dinner mystery theaters.
3. Uses current personnel.	3. Uses fired personnel.	3. Offer on-board career-planning seminars.
4. Returns investment within one year.	4. Becomes the "black hole" of unprofitable investments.	4. Offer continuing education credits for astronomy and other courses.

40. Fairy Tale Time

Story telling is an ancient art dating back to when humans first communicated with words. It has provided most societies with an oral history long before written records were kept. Stories help perpetuate the foundational myths people use to teach succeeding generations about their cultures. For instance, fables, nursery rhymes, and fairy tales have been used to transmit life's lessons to countless people in a number of different cultures.

Although modern technology has diminished its importance, story telling still has the potential to help solve problems. Stories from the past can help suggest ideas for today's problems. Create a story and you create stimuli which can trigger new thoughts and concepts. The richer and more elaborate your story, the richer and more elaborate your stimuli.

One special type of story, with great potential for sparking ideas, is the fairy tale—a story of magical events with a moral. Such stories are excellent sources of idea stimuli for all sorts of problems. The steps are quite simple:

❶ Select a common fairy tale. In case you've forgotten, examples include such Grimm's fairy tales as Rapunzel, Hansel and Grethel, Little Red Riding Hood, Tom Thumb, The Sleeping Beauty, Snow White, and Rumpelstiltskin.

❷ Read the fairy tale and memorize or write down its major elements (e.g., characters, actions, dialogue, plot, morals, events). Or, if you have the time and want to experiment, write your own version of a fairy tale. While reading or writing your tale, try to forget the problem completely. Shut it out of your mind, if you can.

❸ Use elements in the fairy tale as stimuli for triggering ideas.

To illustrate, suppose you're a divisional manager in a medium-size manufacturing firm. You and Jim Oversee—one of your line supervisors—are discussing ways to cut costs. Jim notes that he recently has received increasing numbers of employee theft reports. You decide this is an area in which you could cut costs significantly. You define the problem as, "How might we reduce employee theft?" To help resolve this problem, you decide to write your own version of Cinderella—one of the best-known fairy tales. After some thought, you compose the following story:

> Cinderella, a beautiful young maiden, is treated badly by her two stepsisters. She must do all the cooking and cleaning while they busy themselves with fancy clothes and social events. One day it is announced that the prince is holding a ball to find a wife. The wicked stepsisters are certain the prince will want to select one of them. [So far, so good. Nothing really different here. But then...] Although Cinderella says she would like to go, the stepsisters laugh in her face and tell her to bake a pumpkin pie instead.
>
> The evening of the ball arrives and the stepsisters leave Cinderella to bake her pie. Instead, Cinderella decides to change clothes first. And then she eats some salad with dressing, while dressing. As Cinderella leafs through her meal while bemoaning her fate, her Fairy Godmother (FG) appears and grants her a wish. Cinderella's stepsisters never allowed her to eat her favorite vegetable, so she asks FG to turn her into a rutabaga. FG smirks and tells Cinder that her magic

wand only works with mice and pumpkins. "O.K., fine," says Cinderella as she tosses her salad over her shoulder. "I suppose I shall have to be a pumpkin, then. Mice are not nice."

With a wave of her wand, FG transforms Cinder into a pumpkin. FG waves her wand again and visually-challenged mice materialize to take Cinder to the ball. Off they go into the night. Their goal: the castle ball. Their plan: Sneak into the castle kitchen and offer the pumpkin for dessert.

Being visually challenged, the mice can't see too well, however. Instead of going to the castle, they go to a poor farmer's cottage. The farmer's wife chases away the mice with her carving knife. (Did you ever see such a sight in your life?). Unfortunately, Mrs. Farmer slips on the mice tails and falls on her knife. The farmer rushes in to say goodbye to his dying wife and decides to make a pumpkin pie with the pumpkin the nice mice brought.

The Fairy Godmother has been watching all of this. She sees the farmer raise his dead wife's knife to carve the pumpkin. Suddenly there is a...POOF! The pumpkin turns into a beautiful maiden, thanks to FG. The farmer is awed by Cinder's beauty and asks her to marry him. Cinder agrees and they decide to toast each other with pumpkin punch in the punch bowl.

While he leaves the house to bury his ex-wife, Cinder picks up the dipper and begins to pour some punch into a cup. The dipper slips and crashes to the ground, breaking into two pieces. Cinder panics and picks up one of the pieces, turns on her left slipper, and bolts out the door with the mice in hot pursuit. The farmer hears all the commotion and returns to the cottage in time to see Cinder running away with the not-so-nice mice in pursuit and Cinder holding the remainder of the dipper. He pushes away a lock of his hair and then vows, to no one in particular: "Somehow, someday, I'll find the fair maiden with the glass dipper!"

Based on this story, here are a few sample ideas for reducing employee theft:

 Install hidden video cameras which record everything employees do (from "visually-challenged mice").

❷ Have a subliminal audiotape which periodically reminds employees not to steal (from "stepsisters...tell her to bake a pumpkin pie instead").

❸ Use voice-recognition locks on storage areas where too many keys might exist (from "laugh in her face").

❹ Provide rewards to customers who report incidents of theft (from "they decide to toast each other").

❺ Have weekly tea or coffee breaks where managers solicit theft-reduction ideas (from "pour some punch into a cup").

❻ Install body temperature sensors that notify security whenever an unauthorized employee enters an "off limits" area (from "bolts out the door with the mice in hot pursuit").

❼ Offer a free "makeover" for employees who report shoplifting or theft (from "The pumpkin turns into a beautiful maiden").

❽ Recruit an employee from another division to work undercover and report on theft problems (from "sneak into the castle kitchen").

❾ Install locks with retina identification which works only with certain employees—an alarm sounds if anyone else tries to open the locks (from "her magic wand only works with mice and pumpkins).

❿ Have all employees submit to a voice-stress analyzer to determine if they are telling the truth about theft (from "The farmer rushes in to say goodbye to his dying wife").

41. Idea Links

Idea Links can be a fun brain booster as well as a creative thinking exercise. It is easy to use and can result in many ideas.

The basic process involved is free association. Unlike other free association boosters, however, Idea Links requires you to free-associate in a specific direction beginning with the action verb. The goal is to direct your associations so that you end up with a link to the object. Here's how to do it:

❶ State your problem using an action verb and an object.

❷ Write the verb on the left side of a sheet of paper and the object on the right side.

❸ Draw four one-inch lines to the right of the first word so that the last line ends just before the object word.

❹ Free-associate a word from the verb and write it on the first line.

❺ Continue to free-associate from one word to another, writing each word on one of the lines. Try to make the final word link to the object.

❻ Review all the associations and use them to trigger new ideas.

❼ When you have generated all possible ideas, list new free associations and start again.

If your problem is to improve a table fan, you might set it up as follows:

Improve _____ _____ _____ _____ _____ fan

Next, begin free associating:

Improve *increase* *speed* *car* *traffic* *congestion* fan

Finally, use the free associations to think of ideas. For instance, you might put a fan on wheels to roll around on a table (from "car") or design a fan that blows air in pulses, like a cough (from "congestion").

Here's another example:

Improve   *better*   *butter*   *bread*   *dough*   *blow*   fan

These words prompt ideas such as putting a chemical on the blades to blow scented air (from "butter") and making a fan with gold blades (from "dough").

42. Imagery Mentor

Did you ever have a secret friend to whom you told all your problems? Do you have an inner voice that helps you solve problems? Are they out to get you?

If you answered yes to all three questions, you may want to obtain professional counseling! If you answered yes to the first two questions, you may want to delay treatment. Apparently, many people listen to an inner voice for guidance. For instance, General Douglas MacArthur supposedly conjured up his hero-father for advice on military strategy. The poet Milton called his inner guide "Celestial Patroness" and described how she helped him compose his writings.

I'm not suggesting that we all have a little person living inside us. Instead, I believe we all have subconscious motives, impulses, feelings, and images. All this material has tremendous potential as a vast, untapped reservoir of creativity.

The problem is that we can't access our subconscious on demand. We have no set of commands or buttons we can push to enter our subconscious. Instead, we have to enter it more indirectly.

Michalko (1991) suggests one way to do this: create a personal, internal mentor. Here's a modified version of his procedure:

❶ Release all your tension and try to relax as much as possible.

❷ Visualize a soft, glowing white light surrounding your body. Allow the light to make you feel secure and comfortable.

❸ Think of your favorite place (house, mountain, forest, stream, boat). Visualize yourself walking into this place. Notice all the details. Try to imagine what it looks like. Experience any sounds, textures, or smells. Absorb as much as you can.

❹ Imagine your personal mentor walking toward you. Look closely at his or her face. What are you experiencing? Think of any special feelings or emotions. Include as much detail as possible.

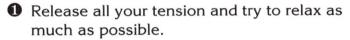

❺ Say to your mentor, "Please be my guide and help me think of new ideas. Lead me in resolving my problem."

❻ Tell your mentor about your problem. Give him or her as much relevant information as you can. Try to keep your interaction realistic. Listen carefully whenever your mentor speaks to you. Don't be discouraged if ideas don't pop out suddenly. It takes time.

❼ Write down any ideas generated during this process. Then end your conversation. Have your mentor say that he or she will be available whenever needed. Experience bonds of trust with your mentor.

It is difficult to fathom the full potential of the human mind and especially the subconscious. We must begin to appreciate its ability to help us resolve problems. Imagery Mentor is a good start.

43. Lotus Blossom

The lotus is a pinkish water lily. As with most flowers, lotus blossom petals are nested together like—well, flower petals. Numerous petals radiate outward from the center, in ever-widening circles. One petal leads to the next and so forth. Just like free association. Perhaps we have the makings of a brain booster here!

Yasuo Matsumura, president of Clover Management Research (Chiba City, Japan) developed the Lotus Blossom method of generating ideas (also called the MY technique, after his Japanese initials). To use this technique, you start with a central theme and then think of an idea. You then use each idea to prompt additional ideas. The specific steps are as follows:

 Write a central theme (problem) in the center of a sheet of paper as shown in Figure 7-3.

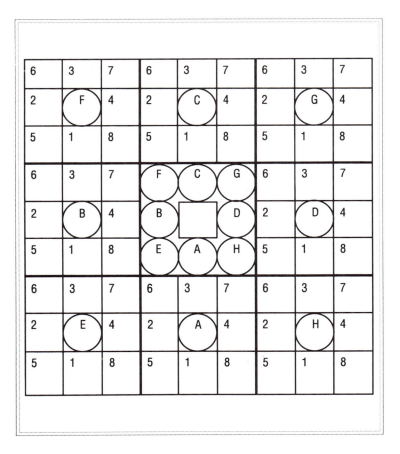

Figure 7-3. Lotus Diagram

❷ Think of related ideas and concepts and write them in the surrounding circles, A through H.

❸ Use each of these ideas as a separate central theme or problem for the surrounding lotus boxes.

❹ Try to generate eight ideas for each of these themes and write them in the surrounding boxes, 1 through 8.

Suppose your problem involves ways to improve a wristwatch. Write "improve a wristwatch" in the center of a sheet of paper. Then write eight related concepts in surrounding circles: (a) watch hands, (b) wrist strap, (c) date, (d) time, (e) second hand, (f) battery, (g) appointments, and (h) face. Next, generate ideas for each of these elements. Here are some examples:

❦ Watch hands—different shapes on ends, different colors, different designs

❦ Wrist strap—buckles, metal, different colors, transparent, different widths

❦ Date—flashing, multicolored, icons for months, written out

❦ Time—voice activated, voice response, flashing lights

❦ Second hand—digital, complementary color, gold plated, variable speed

- Battery—recharge in wall outlet, owner can replace

- Appointments—record appointments, beeper reminder, link appointments with other watches

- Face—celebrity faces, pictures of famous landmarks, spinning

44. Say Cheese

When we first think of new ideas, they often flit about without defined shape. If we really concentrate, we can bring them into focus. These new ideas then become images we can capture in our mind's eye.

Frame. Focus. Click. There the images are. It's almost as if we photograph them with a camera.

VanGundy (1983) used this comparison to suggest a procedure for stimulating ideas using an imaginary camera. The steps are as follows:

1. Imagine you are looking at your problem through the viewfinder of a camera. Frame the picture and adjust the focus to view the entire problem in sharp detail. Move your mind forward or backward to adjust the focus. Add light to improve your view. Then, make the image blurry to change perspective. Finally, add different lenses

such as telephoto or wide angle to change perspectives again. Continue to make adjustments until your problem is centered clearly in your mind's eye.

❷ Push your mental shutter-release button and allow a picture of the problem to develop in your mind. Study the picture and try to absorb all relevant details. Write down any interesting features such as size, shape, texture, smells, movement.

❸ Examine your descriptions and use them to prompt ideas.

45. Sense Making

Our everyday language is colored by references to the five senses: "I hear you," "I see what you mean," "I feel for you," "That's a tasty idea," "I smell a rat!" Such phrases usually prompt a variety of sensory images, corresponding to whatever sense is involved. These images, in turn, help communicate meaning and increase understanding.

Just as our senses allow us to experience different stimuli, sensory images can help us experience the different perspectives needed to create ideas. Here's how to do it:

❶ Try to become as relaxed as possible. Breath comfortably at an even rate. Listen to your breathing and let all stress flow out.

❷ Think about your problem in detail and try to experience it. Quickly smell it, see it, taste it, touch it, and hear it.

❸ Think of your sense of smell. Visualize different olfactory experiences you've had. For instance, you might think about some flowers you once smelled. Now, how might you use your sense of smell to generate ideas to solve your problem?

❹ Think of your sense of sight. Visualize different sight experiences you've had that have affected you emotionally. Now, how might you use your sense of sight to generate ideas to solve your problem?

❺ Continue this process with your senses of taste, touch, and hearing. Think of emotional experiences involving each of these senses. What ideas do these experiences suggest?

To illustrate this method, consider a publisher's problem of how to increase book sales. Here are some ideas that this booster might spark:

- *Smell:* Produce books that contain fragrances that reflect literary themes.

- *Sight:* Include a page of slides to illustrate topics.

- *Taste:* Include free stamps to encourage book buyers to mail in coupons redeemable for discounts on future book purchases.

- *Touch:* Make book covers with different textures that invite people to touch them. Once people pick up a book, they will be more likely to buy it.

- *Hearing:* Put audio-digital computer chips (like those in greeting cards) in the inside covers of books. When someone opens the front cover, the book says, "Buy me, please!"

46. Skybridging

This technique allows you to work both forward and backward when generating ideas. Engineers call this method "reverse engineering." Professional inventor and former engineer Doug Hall (1994) calls it Skybridging.

This booster is based on a general definition of a problem as a gap between a current and a desired state of affairs. That is, you examine "what is" and "what should be" and then try to close the gap by working toward your goal and then back toward the current problem state. There are many different roads to an objective. The steps for Skybridging are as follows:

❶ On the left side of a sheet of paper, define where you are today. If product improvement is your concern, list a current product.

❷ On the right side of the paper, describe where you would like to be. What is the ideal result?

❸ Draw a straight line between the current and desired states. Write on the line a sure thing and a boring thing, both of which represent ways to achieve the desired state.

❹ Draw another connecting line that bends in the middle as shown in Figure 7-4. On the left side of the line, list an obvious idea; on the right side, a safe idea. Continue drawing lines and listing ideas as shown in the figure until you have generated all the ideas you can. (Notice that words on the arches become more impractical the higher you go.)

❺ As you list ideas, try working from right to left on some of the lines.

❻ After you have finished listing ideas, examine them and make the impractical ideas more practical.

Figure 7-4 shows a sample skybridge based on generating ideas for improving a flashlight. The figure suggests several ideas, some directly and some indirectly:

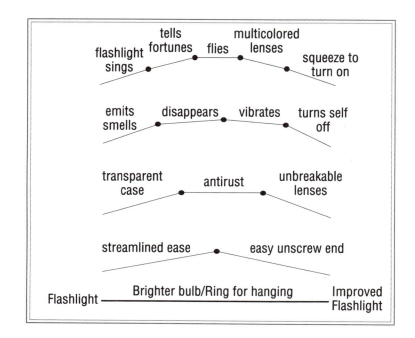

Figure 7-4. Skybridging

47. Tabloid Tales

There you are, in line in the supermarket. The customer at the checkout counter just realized she has to pay for her groceries. She slowly gets out her checkbook and begins writing. After several minutes you notice she has finally written down the date. Unfortunately, it's July and she's had trouble remembering the date change from last year. She wrote down last year's date and has to start over.

You sigh and begin looking around for a distraction. You glance to your left at the magazine rack and you see it: "GIRL, 10, GIVES BIRTH

TO CALF THAT LOOKS LIKE ELVIS." The headline sears into your brain and you shake your head as you struggle to reassert your rationality. You read on:

- ♥ WIFE MAKES SALAD DRESSING OF HUSBAND IN BLENDER

- ♥ BABY BORN WITH THREE HEADS, SIX TAILS, AND BLUE EYES

- ♥ WOMAN DIVORCES FROG—CLAIMS NO PRINCE

- ♥ BIGFOOT SPOTTED DANCING WITH ELVIS

- ♥ MAN GIVES BIRTH TO VW

- ♥ NEW DIET GROWS EXTRA TOES

- ♥ TRUCKER'S LUNG EXPLODES WHILE HE WAS SMOKING ON ROAD

- ♥ ALIENS RESPONSIBLE FOR LIGHT BULB BURNOUTS

You've just been victimized by tabloid headlines. But don't fret. You can salvage something positive from your experience by using tabloid headlines to prompt ideas. Doug Hall (1994) developed Tabloid Tales to help people distort facts and gain new perspectives on their problems. He suggests the following steps:

❶ List four key facts about your problem, product, service, or process.

❷ Distort one aspect of each fact. Make it sensational or more provocative. State it as a tabloid headline.

❸ For inspiration, thumb through a tabloid. (Hall recommends *Weekly World News*.)

❹ Use the distorted facts to generate practical ideas.

To illustrate, suppose you want to reduce auto theft. Four key facts are (1) auto thieves don't want to attract attention, (2) some cars are more likely to be stolen than others, (3) unlocked and unattended cars with running engines are likely theft candidates, and (4) alarms will deter some thieves. These facts suggest the following tabloid headlines:

- ELVIS SEEN HONKING HORNS OF PINK CADILLACS

- CAR THIEF HIDES CAR IN HIS PANTS

- PREVIOUSLY STOLEN CAR DRIVES SELF AWAY FROM THIEF

- STOLEN CAR BLOWS UP CLEVELAND

These headlines then prompt the following ideas:

- Car starts only when driver sings a specified Elvis song.

- Car starts only when driver's rear end fits specially molded car seat.

- Hot-wired cars stop running after one minute.

- Car started without special code sprays knockout gas in face of driver.

48. We Have Met the Problem and It Is Us

A primary counseling skill is empathy—the ability to see and feel something from another's perspective. Some people say you can't really understand how others feel about something unless you crawl under their skin (figuratively, that is, for you followers of the Addams family) and see the world with their eyes. "Change perspectives and you change understanding" is a principle that underlies many brain boosters and applies especially well to this booster.

Try to become your problem and you'll create new perspectives that may help spark new ideas. Of course, you can't literally become your problem (unless you have special powers). You can, however, bring life to your problem and alter how you see it. For this reason, this booster will probably work best with problems involving inanimate objects. This doesn't mean you shouldn't try it with people problems; it just may not be as effective. The steps are as follows:

❶ Think about what your problem would say, think, and feel about itself and its relation to its environment. What bugs it? What does it like? What are its major concerns, challenges, and opportunities?

❷ Write down everything you can think of from step 1.

❸ Use your descriptions as stimuli to think of new ideas.

Here's an example of how to use this booster to improve a wastebasket (the wastebasket is speaking):

> I'm sick and tired of being emptied so often. The food and cigarette ashes smell terrible. I also hate it when people bang me around and leave marks on my outside. It really irritates me when people knock me over and my insides spill out all over the carpet. I just hate all the messes. And they're not even my fault.
>
> There is one nice thing about being a wastebasket. I just love it when some hotshot tries to impress his friends by throwing a paper wad in me from across the room. If the paper wad hits my rim, I sometimes can jiggle a little and knock it to the floor. This makes the hotshot look so foolish!

Based on this diatribe, I think of the following ideas:

- A built-in trash compactor

- A continuous roll of plastic lining that can be removed easily every time the wastebasket is emptied

- A built-in slot for a fragrance dispenser

- Suction cups, clamps, or Velcro for attaching the wastebasket to the floor or a desk to prevent accidental spills

- A basketball-type net that can be raised above the rim for practicing paper wad shots

49. What if...?

What if cows could fly?

What if we grew telephones in our ears?

What if we were all thumbs?

What if diamonds were soft and cushions were rock hard?

What if plants could talk?

What if people who asked "What if...?" all the time suddenly died?

Do you get the idea? As you read each of these questions, images formed in your mind. Most of these images probably were rather provocative. At least, they were a little out of the ordinary. Anytime our minds encounter contradictions or paradoxical thinking, we experience a perspective shift. In this case, asking "What if...?" frees our minds and opens them to possibilities we might never have thought of or explored. Asking "What if...?" pushes out the boundaries of impossibilities and limits.

What if...? is one of the simplest, yet most powerful, brain boosters available. It is often overlooked, however, because it is so simple. Here's how to use this booster:

❶ Stretch your problem in as many ways as you can think of by asking "What if...?" Assume anything is possible. Don't worry about what won't work or why something can't be implemented. Just let your mind go.

❷ Return to reality and examine each question while thinking, "Well, we can't do that, but maybe we can...."

❸ Record all your ideas and make them more practical as needed.

What if you were a car dealer who wanted to increase repeat business? To think of ideas, you might begin "Whatiffing" as follows:

- What if I gave repeat customers a free car?

- What if prospective repeat customers had to beg to let me sell them a new car?

- What if prospective repeat customers tried to pay double the price for a new car?

- What if a customer's current car hypnotized the customer into buying another car?

- What if new cars followed people around town until the people bought them?

Next, use these questions as idea triggers. Here are some sample ideas:

- I can't give repeat customers a free car, but I could give them a substantial discount.

- I can't get repeat customers to beg me to sell them a new car, but I could contact customers on a regular basis to see if they have any problems. Such constant attention may encourage repeat sales.

- I can't double the price for a new car, but I could offer to pay customers double the difference of any better car deal they can get from another dealer.

- A customer's car won't hypnotize the customer into buying another car, but I could mount a relentless advertising campaign using all media.

- New cars won't follow customers around, but I could offer repeat customers free use of a cellular car phone for one year.

CHAPTER
8

Grab Bag

Open the bag. Now reach right in and help yourself. Grab whatever you find. Don't be shy; take a risk and see what you get. You'll never know if you don't try.

A grab bag can't be beat when it comes to surprises. You never know what you're going to get. That also is true of this chapter. You don't know what you're going to get because this chapter contains miscellaneous brain boosters.

Grab bag boosters actually involve two different types of idea stimulators. The first type, "backward," includes boosters that involve reversing or turning around a problem in some way. The second, "just alike only different," contains boosters based on analogical thinking; that is, they generate ideas by focusing on similarities between a problem and something else.

Because these two types of boosters force you to look at your problems differently, these methods are especially useful for creating unique perspectives.

Backward Boosters

Backward boosters stimulate your brain by forcing you to reverse problem aspects and view things differently. This opposite tactic is not what most people expect to use when generating ideas. The typical reaction is to plunge right in and attack a problem by generating solutions— definitely a direct approach.

The point is, however, that reversals avoid the tendency to lock in on just one way of viewing a problem. Divergent, creative thinking requires many problem viewpoints.

50. Law Breaker

Just as most societies have laws, so do most problems. Societal laws prescribe and govern social behavior. Similarly, problem laws govern the assumptions people use to perceive and define problems.

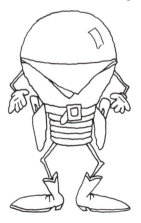

Our assumptions about the way we think things should be influence the way we generate ideas to solve problems. Unfortunately, most of these "shoulds" constrain our thinking and result in less creative ideas. Moreover, shoulds limit the number of solution categories we might consider. For instance, if we accept the notion that chocolate candy should be sold only in bars, all our ideas for chocolate candy will be based on bar products.

BRAIN BOOSTERS FOR BUSINESS ADVANTAGE

To overcome this creative thinking obstacle, Doug Hall (1994) designed Law Breaker as a method to generate ideas by breaking assumptions about the way things should be. The steps are quite simple:

❶ List all possible assumptions about your problem.

❷ Break each assumption. Specifically, ask why the assumption is made about a particular aspect of a problem.

❸ Use the broken assumptions to stimulate new ideas.

To illustrate, suppose you want to generate ideas for a new chocolate candy bar. First, list assumptions regarding candy bars:

- Rectangular bar form

- Solid brown in color

- Uniform sweetness

- Uniform taste

- May contain either peanuts or almonds in addition to chocolate, but nothing else

- Wrapped in aluminum foil

- Melts in the sun

- Weighs no more than three ounces

Next, generate ideas by breaking any of these "laws" governing chocolate candy bars. Here are some possible ideas:

- ♥ Triangular-shaped bar

- ♥ Different shades of brown in the same product

- ♥ Variable sweetness in different parts of the product

- ♥ Different fillings in the center

- ♥ Wrap in "theme" papers (for example, dinosaurs, space travel)

- ♥ High heat resistance

- ♥ Variable weights ranging from one ounce to ten pounds—all with names reflecting the weights (for example, "air" bar, "monster" bar)

51. Reversals

Sometimes we have trouble solving problems because we attack them head-on and become immersed. The result is that we become too close to the problem and find ourselves unable to generate new perspectives.

This can't-see-the-forest-for-the-trees outcome can be avoided by entering the forest from

BRAIN BOOSTERS FOR BUSINESS ADVANTAGE

a different direction. Change direction and you change perspectives. Instead of being blocked by your initial, unproductive perspective, you will discover new ways of seeing your problem. New ideas will then flow.

Problem reversals have been widely used ever since brainstorming was popularized by Alex Osborn in the 1930s. Creativity consultant Edward de Bono (1972) also advocated reversals as one way to achieve his concept of "lateral thinking."

Stand-up comedians and cartoonists often use reversals to create the unexpected. Just look at Gary Larson's "The Far Side." One of his cartoons, for instance, depicts rifle-holding bears hunting people.

Everyday creative problem solving also benefits from reversing a problem statement. A popular approach to law enforcement is to reverse the problem of going out and getting the bad guys. Some police officers instead think of ways to get the bad guys to come to them.

Sounds far-fetched, doesn't it? Why would wanted criminals come to the police? One result of reversing thinking on this problem is for police to send out invitations to a special "party." The "guests" are arrested when they show up. Another is to notify wanted people they have won a prize and must show up in person to claim it. Thus, a simple change in problem definition provides a hot idea.

Reversals also have great potential for all-purpose idea generation. The steps are as follows:

❶ State the problem simply and clearly.

❷ Reverse the direction of the problem statement. This reversal doesn't have to be a direct reversal of any particular problem aspect. You may change the verb, the goal, or any words in the definition. In this regard, reversal is defined broadly as any change in a problem statement.

❸ Write down each reversal as a new (possibly silly-sounding) problem statement.

❹ Use each reversal as a stimulus for new ideas.

Suppose your problem is designing a new soda can. Possible reversals include the following:

- Design an old soda can (classic picture or bottle shape).

- Design a soda bottle.

- Destroy a soda can.

- Design a new beer can.

- Design a new trash can.

Next, use these reversals to help think of ideas:

- A can with a classic logo or picture

- A can in the shape of a bottle

- A can that decomposes after use

- A can with two compartments, with one side containing soda and one beer

- A can that beeps after being emptied until it is deposited in a recycling bin. The beeping stops after sensors are activated when the can is placed in the bin.

52. Turn Around

Turn Around was originally developed by creativity consultant Steve Grossman (1984) as Assumption Reversals. It is a relative of the Law Breaker brain booster [50] and generates ideas by reversing problem assumptions in any way possible. The difference between the two methods is that Law Breaker reverses what is commonly accepted as a "should" about a problem (for example, chocolate should be brown), whereas Turn Around reverses more general assumptions (for example, people eat chocolate).

Some problem assumptions are extremely basic and fundamental, whereas others may be more abstract and esoteric. For instance, a basic assumption of a problem involving attracting new bank customers would be that the customers have money to invest. A more abstract assumption might be that customers put their money in banks primarily to satisfy their needs for security.

Either type of assumption is appropriate for this booster.

For the problem of attracting new bank customers, you might list the following assumptions:

- Potential customers have money.

- Placing money in the bank satisfies security needs.

- Many potential customers are confused by banking procedures.

- Banks loan money to make money.

- People have to wait in line to get money.

- When you withdraw your money, it is not really the same money you deposited originally.

- Banks keep money in vaults.

Next, reverse these assumptions as shown in the following examples:

- Potential customers have no money.

- Putting money in the bank makes people insecure.

- Potential customers all are knowledgeable bankers.

- Banks loan money to lose money.

- People never have to wait to get money.

- Banks keep money in the open.

Finally, use these reversals to suggest ideas:

- Emphasize the lowest-interest loans in town.

- Stress security measures taken to protect the customers' money.

- Develop commercials showing the professional expertise of the bank's officers and staff.

- Give customers who recruit other customers a higher interest rate.

- Offer home ATMs.

- Place a see-through bank vault door in the center of the bank.

Just Alike Only Different Boosters

People who like boosters in the "just alike only different" category will take to them like a duck takes to water or a pig takes to mud. If people really like these boosters, it will be like falling in love for the first time or the joy that comes from the birth of your first child. People may like these boosters because the boosters help them function as smoothly as a fine Swiss watch.

All of the previous paragraph represents analogical thinking—comparisons based on similarities. Whenever you say something is "like" something else, you make an analogy. Such expressions enrich and enliven language and interpersonal communication in particular. Analogies also allow us to express ourselves creatively. Thus, all analogies are creative products.

Analogies can be quite helpful for explaining difficult concepts and solving problems. For instance, educators use analogies extensively when trying to teach difficult concepts. Teachers pick one topic familiar to students and compare it with an unfamiliar topic. This enables students to understand the new topic more clearly based on their familiarity with the first topic. (You may also use analogies when you try to explain a difficult subject to someone.)

Analogies also have broad applicability in the business world. One of the most famous examples involves the use of analogies to develop Pringles Potato Chips. A client of the Cambridge consulting firm Synectics, Inc., gave the firm a problem of how to put more potato chips on supermarket shelves. Regular bags of potato chips contain a lot of air and take up valuable space. If the product could be compressed, the company could increase its sales volume.

To solve this problem, firm members thought of other things in life that are compressed. One that stood out was leaves. When crushed and mixed with water, the leaves would still be there but would use less space. So the firm applied this concept to potato chips by mixing water with dehydrated potatoes, shaping the chips, stacking them, and putting them in small, cylindrical containers. Voila! An elegant solution using analogical thinking.

The boosters that follow are based on this same process of applying analogies, but these methods add a few twists. The only exception is the booster I Like It Like That [55], which provides a more structured approach to analogical thinking.

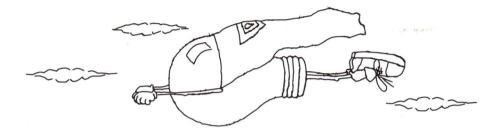

53. Bionic Ideas

Mother Nature is a pretty wise old gal. Among other things, she is a superior problem solver. Think about it. She has resolved countless problems for plants and animals (including humans). Many plants "know" how to turn toward a light source, for instance. And she helped bats to navigate without eyes, snakes to move without legs, and giraffes to eat leaves off tall trees.

One specific type of analogy is known as "bionics." Whereas general analogies reflect similarities anywhere in life, the Bionic Ideas booster looks to Mother Nature for similarities. Why invent the wheel if Mother Nature has already done it?

Research labs have resolved a variety of electronic, thermal, hydraulic, mechanical, and chemical problems using Bionic Ideas. For example, the eye of a beetle was used as an analogy to develop an aircraft ground-speed altitude indicator. Alexander Graham Bell used characteristics of the human ear to invent the telephone, and rattlesnake temperature-sensing organs helped suggest the guidance system for the Sidewinder heat-seeking missile.

One famous analogy involved a product that is analogous to the common cocklebur. A hunter walking through a field noticed how cockleburs caught on his trousers using a hook and loop mechanism. This closure system suggested the concept of Velcro. An entire industry developed from this simple observation.

The steps for Bionic Ideas are as follows:

❶ State the problem as clearly as possible. Use an action verb and an object (for example, how to increase sales).

❷ Describe the major principle or process that underlies the problem. Increasing sales, for instance, involves the principle of getting more of something.

❸ Think of similar principles in nature (that is, biological or botanical analogies).

❹ Use these similar principles or processes to stimulate new ideas.

For instance, suppose you are the manager of a department store. Your assistant has informed you that the store's losses due to shoplifting are greater than ever. To help resolve this problem, you decide to try Bionic Ideas.

You state the problem as "How could we prevent shoplifting in our store?" Next, you describe the major principle or process as prevention. You then make a list of things in nature that involve the concept of prevention:

- ❦ Most birds build their nests in trees to prevent predators from reaching the nests.

- ❦ Some animals change the color of their skin to blend in with their environment and prevent attacks from enemies.

- ❦ Squirrels put away nuts for the winter to prevent starvation during the cold months.

- ❦ Many animal couples take turns guarding their nests to prevent harm to their offspring.

- ❦ Camels store large quantities of water in their bodies to prevent thirst and dehydration.

- ❦ Turtles quickly pull into their shells to prevent predators from biting their head or legs.

- ❦ Mother Nature installs a strong sex drive in most animals to prevent extinction of the species.

- Many plants turn toward a light source to prevent loss of growth (the so-called phototropic response).

- Leaves drop off many trees to prevent the trees from having to provide nourishment during the winter months.

- Many animals make loud noises to prevent enemies from attacking.

These comparisons suggest the following ideas:

- Install cameras in ceilings to watch for shoplifters.

- Have security personnel pose as shoppers to blend in and nab any shoplifters.

- Save extra money to make up for stolen merchandise.

- Have employees rotate turns looking for shoplifters.

- Encourage customers to turn in shoplifters by having a lottery among customers who report shoplifting. The winner receives an ocean cruise.

- Install a sensor so that all the doors close automatically when the device detects that someone is trying to leave the store with stolen merchandise.

- Offer employees rewards to encourage them to help perpetuate profits for the store by catching shoplifters.

- Have all the store's lights begin flashing whenever someone attempts to leave with stolen items.

- "Drop" very expensive items into tall boxes to prevent people from reaching the items. Instead, expensive items must be retrieved electronically by a clerk.

- Install an alarm that sounds whenever someone tries to pick up an item before a clerk has turned off the alarm.

54. Chain Alike

If you generate ideas using analogies, your source of stimulation is generally limited to comparisons with the basic problem principle. For instance, the problem of preventing shoplifting (the Bionic Ideas [53] illustration) is limited to analogies involving the principle of prevention. Although there is nothing wrong with this limitation, it does restrict the number of possible problem perspectives. And that's not good.

Fortunately, all is not lost. The Chain Alike method attacks problems from multiple perspectives. And that's good.

Chain Alike is based on the Attribute Analogy Chains procedure developed by Koberg and Bagnall (1976). You generate ideas by listing problem attributes, developing analogies for each attribute, and then using the analogies to prompt ideas.

Chain Alike is slightly more complicated than other analogy-based boosters. The steps, however, are relatively straightforward:

❶ List all major problem attributes (for example, name, form, parts, shape, structure, processes, materials, functions).

❷ For each attribute, list several subattributes that describe the attributes. Thus, "round" and "square" would be examples of two types of shapes.

❸ Write down several analogies or similar words for each subattribute. The word "round," for example, might spark "circular," "a dog chasing its tail," and "a rolling ball."

❹ Examine each analogy and see what ideas are triggered.

To illustrate Chain Alike, consider the shoplifting problem used for Bionic Ideas. Major problem attributes include the following:

♀ Customers

♀ Merchandise

- Money
- Security
- Observing customers

Next, list subattributes:

Name: Shoplifting

Customers: Children, elderly, middle-aged, rich, poor, educated, uneducated

Merchandise: Electronics in display cases, clothing on shelves and racks.

Money: Dollar bills, coins, credit cards, debt, charging, exchange rates

Security: Guards, cameras, alarms, lighting, electronic sensors

Observing Customers: Watching, unobtrusive, disguises, equipment

Next, look at the subattributes and develop analogies for each one. For instance, some sample analogies might include the following:

Name: Disappearing merchandise

Customers: Small people, money collectors, enhanced brains

Merchandise: Electron organizers, viewing boxes, stacking levels

Money: Circular disks, plastic debits, substituting values

Security: Caretakers, visual image capturing devices, illumination projection

Observing Customers: Hidden recesses, cover-ups, electronic information processors

Finally, generate ideas using these analogies:

- Lock all merchandise in display cases (from "disappearing merchandise").

- Install a system so that people must pay for merchandise on their way out to unlock an exit door. People who don't buy anything subject themselves to personal inspections (from "money collectors").

- Place video cameras on merchandise counters (from "viewing boxes").

- Provide educational seminars in schools on the pitfalls of shoplifting (from "substituting values").

- Place monitors throughout the store that show shoplifters being arrested (from "visual image capturing devices").

- Project onto the walls pictures of previous customers who were caught shoplifting (from "illumination projection").

- Put all merchandise in vending machines (from "hidden recesses").

55. I Like It Like That

This booster is the grandparent of all the just alike only different methods. It is based on general analogical thinking that relies on the direct comparison of one thing or action to another. As with Bionic Ideas [53], you will seek comparisons that might spark ideas. The difference is that you may draw the comparisons from anywhere, not just from Mother Nature.

Once you have identified the similarities, you then elaborate on them and use them to stimulate ideas. The specific steps are as follows:

❶ Think of the major principle underlying the problem and use it to generate a list of things similar to the problem. To help generate this list, say, "This problem is like...."

❷ Select one of the analogies and describe it in detail. Elaborate as much as possible, listing parts, functions, or uses. Be sure to include many action-oriented phrases. If possible, select an analogy that is controversial or out of the ordinary.

❸ Review each description and use it to stimulate ideas.

Suppose you decide to use analogies to help recruit more engineers for your company. The major principle in this case is getting more of something. Thus, you might think of analogies prompted by the phrase "This problem is like..."

- Asking your parents for an increase in your allowance

- Asking your boss for a raise

- Asking a cook for more food

- Asking your boss for more time to complete a project

- An employee trying to get more power over another employee

- A football team trying to win more games

- A panhandler begging for more money

- Calling people to sell more magazines

Select one of these analogies and elaborate.

A panhandler begging for more money involves the following things:

- Deciding which people to ask

- Not being too overbearing

- Watching out for the police

- Looking pathetic

- Using creative requests, such as asking for a quarter to call about graduate school admission

- Looking as presentable as possible

- Maintaining eye contact
- Finding the best location
- Using many different locations

Finally, use the elaborations to suggest ideas for recruiting engineers:

- Screen potential candidates using recommendations and background checks.
- Use a "soft sell" approach; don't seem overly interested.
- Conduct security checks.
- Tell top recruits how much you need them.
- Give prospects a toll-free number to call if they have questions.
- Scout out the best recruiting locations.
- Search for a variety of personality and ability types by recruiting from many different schools in various regions of the country.

Some research suggests that analogies are more likely than other direct stimulation methods to yield unique ideas. Analogies also seem to work especially well for mechanical problems. For instance, analogies have been used to design a new type of thermos bottle closure and a way to attach spacesuit helmets. Although this method may take a little more effort, it is quite useful for difficult problems.

56. What Is It?

Advertising and marketing professionals frequently push products based on assumptions regarding core motivations and needs. Rather than appeal to people to buy a product based on its features, advertisers try to show potential customers how a product will satisfy some need.

For instance, one advertisement might push a brand of coffee because it tastes good. Another, in contrast, might emphasize how the product will satisfy the need to feel secure. Because security may be a stronger motivator than the taste of coffee, consumers may respond more positively to the need-satisfaction approach.

Here are some other possible examples:

- A convertible isn't a car, it's excitement.

- A watch isn't a timepiece, it's a piece of jewelry.

- A job position recruitment campaign isn't for a job, it's for prestige and recognition.

- A coat isn't for warmth, it's a fashion statement.

All of these relate to the question, What is it? Hall (1994) uses this question as the basis for an idea generation method by the same name. You generate ideas by thinking what else your problem is and then using these descriptions as idea stimuli. The steps are as follows:

❶ Describe your problem in at least six different ways.

❷ Use the descriptions to prompt ideas.

To illustrate this simple procedure, consider the problem of improving an office desk. First, describe what desks are. For instance, you might say that office desks are not just desks, they are

- Smooth writing areas
- Occupational centers
- Computer support stands
- Leg and lap covers
- Hollowed-out wooden boxes

Then, use these descriptions to generate ideas:

- A variable-tilt writing surface built into the desk top.
- Desks tailored to different occupations. For instance, a doctor's desk might have a place to hold a stethoscope, a blood pressure cuff, and other diagnostic tools, as well as a built-in computer screen with the *Physician's Desk Reference* on a CD-ROM disk.

- A computer monitor that flips up when needed, a CPU under the desk, and a keyboard built into the desk top.

- A desk with heating pads and foot warmers.

- A desk that can be collapsed easily and stored in a compact area.

PART
3

GROUP
BRAIN
BOOSTERS

The five chapters in this part describe group brain boosters based on either brainstorming (Chapters 9 and 10) or brainwriting (Chapters 11 and 12) procedures. Boosters within these categories are subdivided further according to their use of related (Chapters 9 and 11) or unrelated (Chapters 10 and 12) problem stimuli. All things being equal, unrelated boosters should have a slight edge in their potential to provoke unique ideas.

As you may recall from Chapter 3, brainstorming boosters are based on variations of traditional brainstorming and rely on verbal communication. Brainwriting boosters, in contrast, involve generating ideas in writing. Research has shown that most brainwriting boosters will yield more ideas than brainstorming boosters.

Part 3's group brain boosters include

- Brainstorming using stimuli related to the problem

- Brainstorming using stimuli unrelated to the problem

- Brainwriting using stimuli related to the problem

- Brainwriting using stimuli unrelated to the problem

CHAPTER
9

Brainstorming With Related Boosters

Brainstorming with related boosters is classic brainstorming as developed and popularized by Alex Osborn. It's idea generation that focuses on the problem and uses the ideas of other group members as stimuli. The key to successful brainstorming is adherence to the following brainstorming principles:

❶ *Defer judgment.* Withhold all evaluation of ideas during idea generation. That is, separate generation from evaluation. Once you have listed all possible ideas, then go back and evaluate them. There's a lot of logic behind this principle. First, most groups don't follow it and, as a result, are less than productive. Second, deferring judgment increases the odds of finding at least one good idea. If you spend a lot of time evaluating each idea as you think of it, you may run out of time before you can list all possible ideas. It's a matter of probability.

Finally, separating evaluation from generation helps avoid creating a negative group climate. Idea generation generally is a fun, positive experience. If you stop to criticize each idea as it is proposed, you're interjecting a negative process that disrupts the more positive aspects. Thus, you never may produce a climate healthy enough for effective idea generation. Separate the processes and you'll be amazed at how productive your group can be.

❷ *Quantity breeds quality.* The more ideas you list, the more high-quality ideas you'll get. Again, it's all a matter of probability. Let's assume there is a potential pool of 500 ideas. That's how many ideas you could generate hypothetically if you had all the brains and time in the world. Of these 500 ideas, assume there are 25 you would consider as high quality. If you use the sequential generate-evaluate, generate-evaluate-generate-evaluate cycle, you may get "lucky" and produce a total of 25 ideas during a one-hour brainstorming session. Now, just what are the odds that a majority of these would be the same 25 high-quality ideas? The answer: not very high. The sequential approach relies on pure chance to produce a high quality idea. It is more logical to increase the odds by first listing as many ideas as possible. You always can go back and evaluate them later. Moreover, each idea you list can help spark other ideas. So, if you defer judgment and shoot for quantity, you may produce 125 ideas. Now, what are the odds that one of those is a high-quality one? The answer: very high. You don't need to be a statistician to figure out this one.

❸ *The wilder the better.* Although idea quantity is essential for idea quality, it may not always be sufficient. You always can't rely on the laws of probability. Thus, you need to free your mind and turn off censors and shake off constraints. Shoot for wild, crazy, silly, off-the-wall ideas. These ideas—and the ones they spark—are the ones you need for high-quality, winning ideas. Don't worry about practicality when generating ideas. Remember, you're supposed to separate generation and evaluation. Instead, focus on how many wild ideas you can think of. Some conventional ideas are O.K., too. But don't make a habit of it. Go for the unusual and see what results.

❹ *Combine and improve ideas.* Another way to ensure high-quality ideas is to not let your ideas get lonely. Give them relatives and friends. That is, use your natural powers of free association and see how you can combine an existing idea with another one to form a completely new idea. Or, encourage your ideas to be all they can be. Empower them to use their full potential. Take an existing idea and try to improve it. How

else might it be implemented? What could you substitute, change, reverse, or make larger or smaller? What would make it better? Go for it and you'll increase your IQ (Idea Quotient) and generate better ideas as well. (Osborne, 1963)

57. Be #1

You want to be number one, don't you? Who doesn't? In the business world, it's important to carve out a niche and then work to dominate it.

Hall (1994) describes how you can use this emphasis on being number one to help generate ideas. All you do is list current benefits of some product or process and then transform them into winning, number one ideas. Here are the specific steps for a group:

❶ Together list the current core benefits of your general business category. Include both the trivial and the essential.

❷ In a second column, transform each benefit into its best state. Use the phrase "the best" or a word that ends in "est" (for example, "fastest").

❸ In column three, list ways to achieve this elevated status. These are your ideas.

❹ Repeat these steps by listing, in column one, new benefits that currently do not exist.

To illustrate this booster, consider a problem involving floor cleaners. Examples of current benefits, being the best, and ideas are shown in Table 9-1.

Table 9-1.
Example of Be #1 Brain Booster: Current Benefits

Current Benefits	Being the Best	Ways to Realize (Ideas)
Shines floors	Best shine	Use luminescence
Cleans floors	The best cleaner	Antiseptic, good smell
Easy application	Easiest to apply	New, precise applicator

After generating ideas using current benefits, repeat the process using new benefits. Examples of new benefits, being the best, and ideas are shown in Table 9-2.

Table 9-2.
Example of Be #1 Brain Booster: New Benefits

New Benefits	Being the Best	Ways to Realize (Ideas)
Quick drying	Fastest drying	Dries instantly
Waxes floors	Best cleaner and waxer	Combination product
Easy-to-hold package	Best ergonomic design	Dispenser also cleans

58. Blender

A blender mixes two or more products together to produce something that may not even resemble the original products. Sometimes the final product is better than either of the originals. That's the philosophy behind the Blender brain booster.

According to Warfield, Geschka, and Hamilton (1975), Blender was originally developed by Helmut Schlicksupp at the Battelle Institute in Frankfurt, Germany. His name for the method was SIL, a German acronym meaning Successive Integration of Problem Elements. This booster combines elements of brainwriting and brainstorming, thus taking advantage of the strengths of each. The steps are as follows:

❶ Each person in a small group (four to seven people) individually writes ideas about the problem for five to ten minutes.

❷ Two group members read one of their ideas aloud.

❸ The other group members attempt to integrate (blend) the two ideas into one idea.

❹ A third group member reads an idea and the group attempts to integrate it with the result of step 3 (that is, all three ideas now are integrated, because idea 3 is integrated with the product of ideas 1 and 2).

❺ This process is repeated until all ideas have been read and the group has attempted to integrate them (some ideas may defy integration).

❻ The group stops when the members find an integrated idea acceptable to all.

To illustrate Blender, assume you belong to a group of professional speakers. The group has met to brainstorm ways to improve their speeches. Group members silently generate ideas in writing for about ten minutes. Then, Mary reads her idea: "Ask the audience to submit questions on your topic before you speak."

Next, John reads his idea: "Tell an opening story to get the attention of the audience and to illustrate your major theme."

The group members think about these ideas and integrate them into one idea: "Ask the audience to submit brief stories illustrating a theme, take a break to analyze their responses, and then tell them the outcome."

After everyone agrees on this idea, Fred reads his idea: "Have audience members pair up with one other person to introduce themselves."

The group members attempt to integrate this idea and come up with this: "To illustrate how people miscommunicate, tell one audience member in a row a 'secret' and have that person tell it to the next person in the row who tells it to the next person and so forth. After the secret makes it to the end of the row, ask the last person to tell the entire audience the secret. The final version of the 'secret' usually is a gross distortion of the original."

Melvin then suggests his idea: "Project your image on screens around the room."

The group attempts to integrate this idea and comes up with the following: "Continually project audience members' facial reactions on a screen to demonstrate feedback through nonverbal communication."

One disadvantage of this procedure is that it may be difficult to integrate all the ideas. This problem can be avoided to some extent by ensuring that all group members understand the problem clearly. If an idea seems incompatible, discard it and try another one.

Sometimes a group will have trouble integrating most of the ideas. When this occurs, the group can record each integration as a separate idea. Regardless of the difficulty of integrating ideas, each idea itself may serve as a standalone solution.

59. Drawing Room

You have probably browsed in a museum at one time or another. As I write this, I have just returned from an art museum in Washington, D.C. (the Phillips Collection). I was struck with the variety of ideas expressed by the paintings from different periods: a Picasso from his blue period communicated some degree of depression, a Renoir showed a group of people enjoying themselves at a boating party luncheon, and a Degas showed ballet dancers preparing to perform. Of course, these are just my subjective impressions. You may not agree with what I see and experience. And that's just fine. The paintings provide rich sources of stimulation to help us interpret and understand our world.

Groups can use this principle of visual stimulation to generate ideas and have fun at the same time. The steps are as follow:

❶ Each group member individually draws a picture representing a solution to the problem. The picture may be either abstract or realistic. It may be best to have one-half of the group draw an abstract version and the other half a more realistic representation. If possible, the group should have crayons to add some color.

❷ Group members tape their pictures to the walls.

❸ Everyone walks around the room and examines the drawings just as people would do in a museum. As group members examine the pictures, they write down any comments or new ideas triggered.

❹ The group reconvenes and uses the drawings as stimuli for new ideas.

60. Get Real!!

We've all heard it before: "That's the stupidest idea I've ever heard!" "It'll never work!" "That's pretty dumb." "Get real!!" We seem to be conditioned to react negatively whenever we hear a new idea. Sometimes, the more innovative the idea, the more repulsed we are. It's as if our attitude is "If I haven't heard of it (or thought of it) before, then it can't be any good" (the "not- invented-here syndrome").

Well, get real! Such a negative attitude isn't going to benefit you or any group. In fact, this attitude can establish a negative climate that eliminates the possibility of developing any useful, innovative ideas.

There is a bright side to such an attitude, however. It can be turned around and used to stimulate ideas. And that's how the Get Real!! booster works:

❶ After a brainstorming session, group members select the two or three stupidest, most impractical, and most unworkable ideas.

❷ Members then examine each of these ideas and see what smart, practical, workable ideas the original ideas might stimulate.

Suppose your company wants to attract people to its financial planning seminars. You and some others brainstorm some ideas and select two of the worst ones:

- 🔦 Call all the people in town and ask them to attend.

- 🔦 Offer to pick people up and drive them to the seminar.

With these ideas as stimuli, the group generates some more practical ideas:

- 🔦 Hire a marketing firm to call people most likely to benefit from such a seminar.

- 🔦 Advertise on a radio show and offer a discount to the first twenty people who enroll by phone.

- 🔦 Pay mileage to seminar participants.

- 🔦 Lease buses to transport people from a common collection point.

- 🔦 Raffle off a free rental car at the seminar.

61. Idea Showers

Let the ideas rain on down. Flood your group with thoughts about how to solve your problem. Try for as much conceptual precipitation as you can generate. It's time for Idea Showers.

Ideas Showers is another name for the classic brainstorming method developed years ago by advertising executive Alex Osborn (1963). As discussed in the introduction, Osborn's four principles are

- Defer judgment
- Quantity breeds quality
- The wilder the better
- Combination and improvement are sought

The trick is to translate these principles into workable brainstorming behaviors. The first principle suggests that groups should agree to think of all the ideas they can before evaluating any ideas. If a group adheres to this principle, they also should be successful with the second principle of quantity breeds quality. Separating generation from evaluation has been found to increase idea quantity, with a corresponding increase in quality. The third principle reinforces the second in that letting go and not being concerned with idea practicality is likely to increase idea quantity. Finally, the fourth principle—combination and improvement are sought—is likely to improve idea quality. Building on others' ideas helps improve existing ideas while triggering new ones.

62. Modular Brainstorming

You've certainly heard the expression "A picture is worth a thousand words." Well, you might also say that a picture is worth a thousand ideas.

Modular Brainstorming (also called Component Detailing) was developed by Wakin (1985) to take advantage of the natural human tendency to use visualization during problem solving. This technique also helps provoke unique perspectives by positioning the pictures in a certain way. The steps are as follows:

❶ Group members generate a list of major problem components and subattributes for each component.

❷ Each group member selects (or is assigned) a different component. If the problem involves a tangible product, members might be given an actual product.

❸ Individual group members study the component and its attributes, noting all details.

❹ Individual members draw a picture of their assigned components, being sure to include as much detail as possible.

❺ The drawings are collected and attached to a wall or board or laid out on a large table. The pictures are arranged so that their placement approximates the components of the actual problem.

❻ The members of the group then examine this collage to stimulate new ideas or improvements. The individual drawings typically vary in size and proportion, thus instantly creating new perspectives.

Wakin has used a common door lock to illustrate this method. Group members first list components such as knobs, latches, pins, tumblers, keys, bolts, springs, and a striking plate. Next, they list subattributes of each component. For instance, springs have such characteristics as being spiral in shape, under tension, capable of being stretched, and varied in size.

After group members draw pictures of the individual components, they arrange the pictures together and examine the collage for stimulation. Thus, the doorknob might suggest a new shape for a handle, and the bolt might be made larger and be designed to interlock with a different mechanism in the doorjamb.

63. Pass the Hat

Doug Hall (1994) uses Pass the Hat as a combination brainstorming/brainwriting procedure for two or more groups. Unlike some brainwriting methods, this booster involves generating problem attributes for stimuli instead of generating ideas. Other groups then used the attributes to spark ideas.

This method emphasizes blending together problem features to produce something new. This "mix and match" process has been around for a while. Consider, for instance, such products as wine coolers that blend wine and fruit juice.

The steps for this technique are as follows:

❶ Each small group receives a silly hat. If you don't have any hats, don't throw your arms up in despair and quit. Instead, try to be creative. Use small paper bags, waste-baskets, plastic sacks, or pillow cases. (Of course, you'll then need to change the name to "Pass the Plastic Sacks" or "Pass the Pillow Cases" or whatever.)

❷ Each group writes, on one slip of paper, five problem attributes, characteristics, emotions, general perceptions, traits, features, or benefits. If there is more than one problem category (for example, different types of beverages such as punch, soda, and milk), the group should complete one list for each category, but no more than a total of three.

❸ Each group places its list into a hat and passes the hat to another group.

❹ Each group uses the list it just received to think of ideas. When a group has finished with the list, the group returns it to the hat and passes the hat to another group, which then uses the list for stimulation.

❺ After the groups have used all the available lists or time is called, the procedure is stopped. (A time limit will generally be needed only when there are multiple lists.)

As an example, suppose you are concerned with packaging and marketing water in plastic bottles. Your group lists five attributes of this product:

❶ The bottle has a screw-on cap.

❷ The water is perceived as being pure and free from contamination.

❸ The bottle can easily be recycled.

❹ Different flavors will enhance the taste of the water.

❺ The bottle is unbreakable and lighter than a glass bottle.

You place this list in a hat and pass it to the next group. This group examines the list and generates the following ideas:

♥ Design a novelty bottle shaped like a water faucet.

♥ Stress product purity in advertisements and label designs.

♥ Demonstrate environmental awareness by providing recycling instructions on the label.

- Use different colors of plastic that match different flavors.

- Package water in bottles shaped like the fruit used to flavor the water.

- Advertise by dropping plastic and glass bottles on a hard surface.

Although Pass the Hat was originally developed for use with multiple groups, it will also work with just one group. Simply use the list you generate instead of one passed to you by another group.

64. Phillips 66

Does the name of this booster make you want to gas up your car? Do you have a sudden urge to buy stock in an oil company? If you answered "yes" to either of these questions, you may be a little strange.

The Phillips 66 method has nothing to do with gasoline, the Phillips Petroleum Company, or your personality. It has a lot to do, however, with the name of the person who devised this booster: Donald Phillips.

Phillips (1948), a former president of Hillsdale College, created Phillips 66 (also known as the Phillips 66 Buzz Session) to help increase audience participation in large groups. Although the method has different variations, the basic steps are as follows:

❶ A large group divides into smaller groups of six people each.

❷ The groups isolate themselves and elect a discussion leader and a secretary/recorder who records and reports the group's ideas.

❸ Each group receives a carefully worded problem statement. This statement usually is the same for each group, although groups could be given different parts of a problem to resolve.

❹ The groups generate ideas for six minutes. (If more time is available, groups should be allowed at least twenty to thirty minutes.)

❺ Each group evaluates its ideas and selects the best ones.

❻ The groups return to their original location and the spokesperson for each group reads aloud the group's best ideas. The conference leader records these ideas.

❼ The final idea list is given to an individual or committee for additional evaluation, or the larger group may discuss the ideas if time permits.

65. Play by Play

Play by Play is another Doug Hall (1994) brainchild that he describes as a step-by-step adventure. This method is much like doing your own minicommercial for television. To pull it off, you'll

need a camera capable of producing instant pictures. Then follow these steps:

 Photograph each step involved in using a
product or process. Start from as far back
as possible and try to go far into the future.

❷ After you've taken all the pictures, arrange
them in order and examine them. Look for
moments that might be improved, moments that seem to have best captured the
essence of your product or process, and the
most intriguing moments.

❸ Redo any pictures that need improvement.

❹ Examine all the pictures again and use
them to help generate new ideas.

For instance, if you manufacture soup and want
to improve business, you might create scenes in
which a small child is shown

 Walking into a kitchen

❢ Pushing a chair toward a cabinet

❢ Smiling as she reaches for a can of soup
in the cabinet

❢ Retrieving a can opener from a drawer

❢ Opening the can of soup with her tongue
projecting from one corner of her mouth

❢ Retrieving a pan from underneath a
counter

- Pouring soup into the pan
- Stirring the soup
- Ladling the soup into a bowl
- Eating the soup with it dripping from her mouth
- Drinking the soup from the bowl
- Sitting and smiling

With these pictures as stimuli, the soup company brainstorming group might think of the following types of ideas:

- Easy-open cans for children
- "Cartoon" soups with appropriate themes and pictures
- A soup can with a built-in heating pan
- A can with a pour spout
- A can with a built-in or attached "classic" soup spoon
- Ready-to-eat cold soups with straws
- Soup cans with small mirrors on the label in which a child's face can be seen as the head of some cartoon character

66. Rice Storm

Not all brain boosters help all people. If one booster doesn't seem helpful, try another. But if you find yourself totally stumped during idea generation, it may be time to back up instead of plunging blindly ahead with more ideas. The solution may not be trying more boosters or finding more creative people. Instead, you may need to devote some time to ensuring the problem is understood.

This need for clarifying a problem is especially critical in groups. The more people involved in problem solving, the greater the number of perceptions that must be dealt with. Each individual may see a problem from a different perspective. In such situations, the group won't be able to generate ideas until all group members are aligned in their perceptions.

Rice Storm (also called the TKJ method) is a Japanese booster developed by Kobayashi and Kawakita. According to Michalko (1991), Rice Storm has two stages: (1) understanding the problem, and (2) solving the problem. Understanding involves ensuring that each group member grasps the essence of the problem; solving involves encouraging individuals to participate in idea generation. The steps are as follows:

Problem Definition

❶ Group members write pertinent facts about the problem on index cards (one fact per card).

❷ The cards are collected and redistributed among the group members so that no one receives his or her original card.

❸ The group leader reads one card aloud.

❹ Group members select facts on their cards that are related to the one read. They then read these facts aloud to the other members, thus building a set of facts.

❺ The group labels the set of facts using a name that reflects the set's essence. The name is derived by considering all the facts and then boiling them down to extract essential features. This name must

    a. Be verifiable using the facts from which it was generated

    b. Be specific (not too general)

    c. Not be a simple combination of the subset of facts

❻ This process continues until all the facts have been distilled into name sets.

❼ Finally, the group members combine all the sets until there is one all-inclusive group of sets that is then named. This name must reflect the essence of the all-inclusive problem definition set. The final set should include all of the previously discussed facts and essences. Group members should affirm this final definition and feel that a consensus has been reached.

Problem Solution

 Group members individually write potential solutions on index cards (one solution per card).

❷ The group leader collects and redistributes the cards so that no one receives his or her original card.

❸ The leader reads one of the solutions aloud.

❹ Group members look over the solutions on their cards and select the ones related to the solution just read. The members then share these related solutions and use them to build solution-set card piles.

❺ The group names each set and places a name card on it. This process continues until an all-inclusive solution set is achieved. The essence of this final solution should incorporate all the previous solutions. Its name should capture the essence of all the solutions.

❻ Finally, the leader asks the group, "What is the essence of the properties and characteristics that are indispensable to these ideas?" This question should trigger new ideas. The leader may then select and

combine the best suggestions into a final solution set.

To illustrate Rice Storm, Michalko describes how a group of computer specialists used this method to consider ways to improve the home computer. The group members first listed verifiable, relevant problem facts:

- We can produce computers that operate twenty to fifty times faster than standard computers.

- Computer screens can be mounted on walls.

- Fiber optics makes higher resolution possible.

- Full-motion video can be mixed with computer graphics.

- Laptops are becoming more portable.

After considering these and other facts, the group described the essence of its challenge as follows: "In what ways might we develop a home computer that is faster, multiuse, multimedia, and high resolution with multiscreens for a variety of purposes?"

Next, group members individually generated ideas. The following ideas were suggested:

- A portable computer so small that you could carry it while holding two bags of groceries.

- A merger of video and computer capabilities with a very high bandwidth link for video access to every movie ever made.

- Electronic publishing involving home computer access to data banks about education, travel, medicine, sports, and so on.

- Cellular transponders in wall outlets to permit placement of computer screens anywhere, allowing movies to be embedded in such novel objects as desks or work areas.

These and other solutions were grouped into sets, named, renamed, and grouped again into an all-solution set that best described the essence of all the previous solutions: "A home multimedia Roger Rabbit." This solution involves a home computer networking system with such features as entertainment (access to every movie ever made); handwriting machines that transfer thoughts automatically to the computer; a scanner; smart software agents to scan databases for useful information and store it in the computer; and custom-designed screens that can be embedded in desks, hung on walls, or carried around.

67. Spin the Bottle

Around and around it goes. Where it stops, only the bottle knows. Do you remember playing spin

the bottle as a child (or even as an adult)? The Spin the Bottle booster is very similar, except you don't have to kiss anyone. Instead, groups use a bottle to point to someone who must then suggest an idea.

According to Hall (1994), who created this booster, Spin the Bottle works like this:

❶ The group leader obtains several empty bottles. Hall recommends regular longneck bottles (or light beer bottles for "less substantial ideas").

❷ Each small group sits on the floor in a circle with a bottle in the center, lying on its side.

❸ One of the group members spins the bottle. The person to whom the bottle points must suggest an idea.

❹ The group discusses the idea for 107 seconds and tries to use it as a springboard for additional ideas.

❺ The person who suggested the previous idea spins the bottle and the group repeats steps 3 and 4 until everyone has suggested several ideas.

68. Story Boards

Story Boards originated with Walt Disney, who created series of pictures to illustrate major scenes during animated films. Each scene was then used as a point around which a complete story could be built. A variety of related procedures for generating ideas has evolved since then. Although there are significant differences among these procedures, these methods all share the common feature begun by Walt Disney: laying out key concepts that are linked together to form a complete whole. The following is typical of many story boarding methods:

❶ Group members brainstorm solution categories (attributes) and write each one on a large card.

❷ Group members use each category as a stimulus for problem solutions and write these solutions on cards.

❸ The solution cards are taped or pinned under the appropriate category card.

❹ Group members examine the solutions and try to generate additional ideas from them or combine solutions across categories and use them as stimuli for new ideas.

❺ The process continues until the group generates a sufficient number of ideas (or time is called).

Suppose you are an automobile manufacturer and your problem is developing ways to reduce auto theft. You get together a group of your best engineers and decide to use Story Boards. You generate problem attributes and write them on cards as shown in Figure 9-1. Next, you use each category to help stimulate ideas. Finally, you examine all the solutions and see what new solutions might be suggested.

The nine ideas listed in Figure 9-1 suggest additional solutions when combined. For instance, someone who tries to break a window might receive a shock (from "break-proof glass" and "car shocks when touched"). Or the car might automatically photograph anyone who walks within five feet of it (from "flashing lights" and "automated voices").

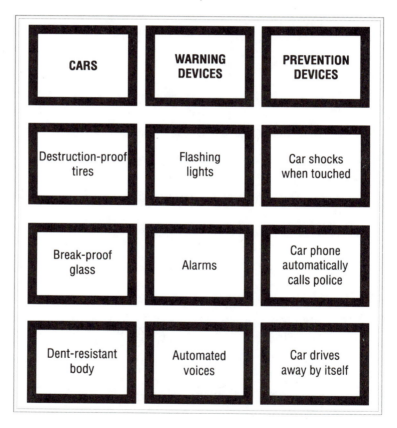

Figure 9-1. Story Boards

BRAIN BOOSTERS FOR BUSINESS ADVANTAGE

69. That's the Ticket!

This booster is the ticket to enhancing your group's creativity. And it's well worth the price of admission. All you have to do is turn in your tickets and watch the ideas flow. It's as simple as that. That's the Ticket! is a relatively uncomplicated brainstorming variation I recently developed. The steps are as follows:

❶ Each group member receives ten blank tickets. (Blank tickets are available at novelty stores and many party shops. Tickets can also be made out of blank pieces of paper or index cards. Each ticket should be approximately one inch by three inches.)

❷ Group members write one idea on each ticket.

❸ All the tickets are placed in the center of a table.

❹ One group member withdraws two tickets and reads them aloud to the group.

❺ The group uses the combination of the two ideas as possible stimulation for new ideas.

❻ The original tickets are returned to the middle of the table and another group member selects two more tickets.

❼ The process of choosing tickets and generating ideas is repeated until all group members have selected two tickets at least once.

Suppose your problem involves improving a telephone. Two ideas might be (1) a padded earpiece, and (2) a built-in radio that either listener can hear if put on hold. These two ideas together suggest the idea of a built-in radio with volume control (from "padded earpiece," which suggests the concept of making something soft).

This booster combines elements of both brainwriting and brainstorming. One useful feature is that you are guaranteed at least ten ideas per group member (assuming each member follows the instructions.) Thus, if you have five group members, you'll get at least fifty ideas before beginning brainstorming.

70. What's the Problem?

"So, exactly what is the problem?" That's a frequently heard sentence in brainstorming groups as they struggle to analyze and define a problem. Groups should devote considerable time to understanding the problem before generating ideas. But by then, it may be too late. They've already corrupted any potential ideas.

Creative problem solving is a "darned if you do, darned if you don't" situation. Defining problems and generating ideas often lead to a paradox. Effective creative problem solving demands that you analyze and define a problem to ensure that you start from the most productive perspective. There is nothing inherently wrong with this. Things get challenging, however, when you start generating ideas following extensive analysis and redefinition.

The more you analyze a problem, the more you understand it. The more you understand it, the closer and more involved you become. Although these outcomes may produce fresh perspectives, they also limit your ability to generate unique ideas. Too much problem knowledge tends to lead to conventional, mundane solution proposals. Another case of a little knowledge being a dangerous thing.

To overcome this problem, William Gordon (1961), a cofounder of the Synectics consulting firm, developed this booster. What's the Problem? attempts to counter our natural tendency to exhaust all conventional solutions and then declare we have run out of ideas. Because Gordon developed his procedure while working at the Arthur D. Little consulting firm, VanGundy (1988) referred to Gordon's procedure as the Gordon/Little method. Taylor (1961) describes the steps as follows:

❶ The group leader describes a general, abstract problem without revealing the "real" problem. This abstract problem should describe the general principle underlying the real problem.

❷ The leader asks the group members to generate ideas for the abstract problem.

❸ The leader describes a slightly less abstract, more specific version of the real problem and asks the group to generate ideas for it.

❹ The leader describes an even more specific version of the real problem and asks the group to generate ideas for it.

❺ The leader reveals the real problem and instructs the group members to examine the ideas for the two abstract problems and use them as stimuli for new ideas.

To illustrate this booster, suppose the problem involves ways to develop a snack that would surprise children. The group leader might first ask the group to think of ways to catch people's attention. The group might make the following suggestions:

- Tap them on the shoulder.
- Yell at them.
- Expose yourself to them.

Next, the leader asks the group to think of ways to shock people. They suggest these ideas:

- Electrocute them.
- Urinate in public.
- Swear at them.
- Do something sexually provocative.

Then the leader asks the group to think of ways to surprise children—a problem even more closely related to the real problem. For this problem, the group generates such ideas as

- Play peekaboo.
- Short-sheet their beds.
- Burst a balloon.

Finally, the leader reveals the problem and asks the group to use all the ideas as stimuli to generate new ideas:

❶ When a child unwraps candy, a scary face appears (from "peek-a-boo").

❷ A telescopic candy bar (from "short-sheet their beds").

❸ Insert a small voice box in candy that yells "ouch!" when bitten (from "yell at them").

❹ Candy-coated small balloons that burst harmlessly when eaten (from "burst a balloon").

❺ Candy shaped like a toilet bowl (from "urinate in public").

10

Brainstorming With Unrelated Boosters

Unrelated boosters are idea generation methods that use unrelated problem stimuli. For some problems and some groups, brainstorming with unrelated boosters may result in better ideas. Unrelated stimuli can help create different perspectives, because these stimuli are not too similar to the problem. (All the tickler boosters in Chapter 5 rely on unrelated stimuli, so they may also produce higher-quality solutions.)

Remember the old saying "You can't see the forest for the trees"? Well, in this case, the trees are problem elements that encourage you to focus all your attention on the problem. This narrow focus limits your perspectives and may actually make it more difficult to generate creative ideas.

Although unrelated stimuli may help you generate better ideas, there is no guarantee. Many other factors also are involved. Problem-solving success is determined by the type of problem, the degree to which it is understood and structured, and the personalities and creative abilities of the group members. Nevertheless, the unrelated boosters in this chapter will increase your odds of getting unique ideas.

71. Battle of the Sexes

Gender wars rage all around us—at least in the minds of people who pay attention to such things. Regardless of your interest in the battle of the sexes, gender differences play a significant role in many areas of life as women strive to gain equality. Gender differences are, of course, not necessarily bad. Remember, "Vive la difference!"

Males and females can make unique contributions in many situations, including creative problem solving. And, that's exactly what Doug Hall had in mind when he developed this booster. Here's how to implement it:

❶ The leader divides a large group into smaller groups of all women and all men. (Although it may not work quite as well, you could use mixed-gender groups if the members of one gender try to adopt the attitudes of the majority gender in the group.)

❷ The leader instructs the group members to generate two ideas using these criteria:

    a. The perfect solution from the perspective of their gender.

b. The perfect solution from the perspective of the opposite gender.

❸ To help the groups generate ideas, the leader gives the male groups a variety of male-oriented magazines such as *Esquire, Field & Stream,* and *Men's Health.* The female groups receive several women's magazines such as *Redbook, Cosmopolitan,* and *Mademoiselle.* The groups look through the magazines and examine words and pictures for potential idea stimulation.

❹ The male and female groups then share their best ideas and the larger group tries to make these ideas more workable or suggests additional ideas.

So, exactly how does this booster work? Well, consider a problem of how to decrease employee absenteeism. The female groups might suggest "feminine" ideas such as holding teas to develop support systems and "masculine" ideas such as organized company sports teams. The male groups might suggest "masculine" ideas such as having managers and workers socialize in bars after work and "feminine" ideas such as sewing circles during lunch periods. Although some or all of the ideas might not be practical, all group participants would then develop more workable solutions.

A nice feature of this booster is that it helps promote healthy competition between the groups. Moreover, both groups often generate ideas based on gender stereotypes, which creates usually friendly conflict. This conflict then serves to motivate the groups and can result in a greater number of ideas. Caution must be used, however, to ensure that the brainstorming session does not become overly sexist.

72. Best of...

Remember how some children grow up taunting their friends that their father is smarter, stronger, richer, or nicer than someone else's father? Or have you noticed how athletes on television point their index fingers upward while chanting, "We're number one"?

Our society seems to have an insatiable appetite for the best of everything. Hall (1994), creator of this booster, once conducted a computer search of newspaper abstracts from 1991 and 1992 and found more than eleven thousand instances of headlines containing the word "best." Every day some television show or magazine bombards us with a "Top Ten" list or other ratings of movies, books, plays, and music. We're a people obsessed with who is best.

One benefit of these "best of" lists is that they have value as idea stimulators. According to Hall, brainstorming groups can use such lists to generate ideas by following these steps:

Group members collect a variety of "best of" lists. The lists may or may not be related to the problem, and they don't need to be "official." If group members don't have access to official lists, they may generate their own lists by reading movie reviews or just brainstorming the best books of the year, the best cars, and so forth.

 The group selects one of the lists and generates traits that make each item a certifiable best.

 The group uses the traits for each item to spark ideas.

❹ The group repeats steps 2 and 3 until it has generated a sufficient number of ideas.

To illustrate this booster, Hall uses the example of inventing a new coat hanger. One of the lists involves Top Ten television shows of the last several years:

♥ **Top TV Show:** Roseanne

Traits: Irreverent, loud, earthy, big, salty, disrespectful, working-class family

Ideas: Extra-strength coat hangers for large or bulky clothes

♥ **Top TV Show:** Cheers

Traits: Friends, leisure time, flippant, beer, sports

Ideas: Hangers with built-in deodorant properties for hanging sweat clothes in lockers

- **Top TV Show:** 60 Minutes

  Traits: Exposes, shocks, champion of the little person, ambushes, confronting

  Ideas: A hanger with a heating tube that dries clothes still wet from the wash, thereby eliminating scandalous shrinkage and the blight of dryer wrinkles

73. Brain Splitter

More than a decade ago, the darling of pop psychology and management psychobabble was the concept of left- and right-brain thinking. Although much of the literature exaggerated or misunderstood how the brain hemispheres actually function during thinking, the basic processes are relatively straightforward.

The right brain is considered the seat of creative, holistic, artistic, nonlinear thinking; the left is the center of logical, analytical, unartistic, linear thinking. The right brain is emotional,

BRAIN BOOSTERS FOR BUSINESS ADVANTAGE

disorderly, experiential, subjective, nonjudgmental, fantasy-like, and concerned with spatial relations and metaphorical meanings. The left brain, in contrast, is more rational, orderly, intellectual, objective, judgmental, realistic, and concerned with verbal relations and literal meanings.

We all have right- and left-brain hemispheres. Although there is evidence that many people have developed certain hemispheric functions more highly than others, no normal, healthy human is truly a left- or right-brain person. The human mind relies on both hemispheres to think and solve problems. The structure that transfers information between the hemispheres is a bundle of nerve fibers known as the "corpus collosum."

You may wonder what all this has to do with brainstorming ideas in groups. Well, you can use the stereotypical aspects of brain functions to prompt ideas. And it can be a fun experience. Here's a slightly modified version of how Van-Gundy (1983) describes the procedure:

❶ The group leader divides a relatively large group into two smaller groups based on their professed right- or left-brain dominance. The leader may choose to administer questionnaires to determine brain orientation, but it's a lot easier just to ask people. This is not a scientific experiment!

❷ The leader instructs the left-brain group members to generate as many practical,

conventional, and logical ideas as they can in twenty minutes.

❸ The leader tells the right-brainers to generate as many far-out, unconventional, and nonlogical ideas as they can in twenty minutes. At least two members in each group should record ideas.

❹ One-half of the members from each group move to the other group. There should now be two groups composed of one-half left-brain thinkers and one-half right-brainers. These groups now represent the corpus collosum function of the human brain.

❺ Each group gives the other a copy of its idea list, so that each has one list of left-brain ideas and one list of right-brain ideas.

❻ The groups randomly select one idea from each list and use the combination to help think of new ideas (sometimes the ideas will come from just one of the lists, and that's O.K., too).

To illustrate Brain Splitter, assume you manufacture umbrellas and want to develop improved designs and features. First, the groups generate two lists:

Left-Brain Ideas

❶ Use a more durable fabric.

❷ Strengthen metal supports.

❸ Design the handle like a pistol grip.

❹ Improve the ability of fabric to shed water.

❺ Use less expensive materials.

Right-Brain Ideas

❻ Create an umbrella that automatically opens when wet and closes when dry.

❼ Add air jets that blow down from the top edges of the umbrella to keep rain off the lower body.

❽ Create an umbrella that repels rain before it hits the fabric.

❾ Make an umbrella that is small enough to carry in a wallet.

The groups combine ideas from each list to produce the following ideas:

Combination Ideas

- 1/6: Develop a faster-drying fabric.

- 1/8: Make an umbrella that vibrates off water.

- 1/9: Make a wallet that doubles as an umbrella.

- 2/7: Put air jets in the ends of the metal spikes to rotate the umbrella automatically, throwing off water.

- 2/8: Eliminate the need for metal supports.

- 2/9: Develop a carrying device designed like a hip or shoulder holster.

- 3/6: Use compressed-air capsules to open the umbrella.

- 3/9: Have the umbrella double as a pistol.

- 4/5: Develop an inexpensive fabric that can be replaced easily when damaged.

- 4/7: Build in air pockets so the umbrella can double as a flotation device.

- 4/8: Eliminate fabric and use only air jets to repel water.

- 5/9: Design a plastic, foldable parka with an umbrella hat.

74. Force-Fit Game

Even the best groups sometimes have trouble generating ideas. Brain boosters usually help when this occurs. There are times, however, when even basic idea generation methods fail, such as when a group simply lacks the necessary motivation. Thus, it's not so much the fault of the booster as the "boostee."

One way to motivate groups under these circumstances is to introduce a little friendly competition. Brain Splitter [73] does this a little, but competition is not included as a basic mechanism. (Force-Fit Game is similar to Brain Splitter, however, in that each booster generates ideas from stimulation provided by both practical and impractical ideas.) To ensure competition, you have to use a procedure based on competitive elements. And that's exactly what the Force-Fit Game does.

According to the booster's developer, Helmut Schlicksupp (in Warfield, Geschka, and Hamilton, 1975), the steps are as follows:

❶ A large group is divided randomly into two small groups.

❷ One person who is not a member of either group assumes the role of referee/recorder.

❸ One group starts by suggesting an idea that is silly or remote from the problem.

❹ The second group is given two minutes to develop a practical solution from this idea.

❺ The referee/recorder writes down the idea and awards the second group one point if he or she judges the idea to be practical; if the referee/recorder determines the group was unsuccessful, he or she gives the first group the point.

❻ After thirty minutes, the referee/recorder declares the group with the most points the winner.

75. Grab Bag Forced Association

This booster is similar to Tickler Things [21], except Hall (1994) modified it for groups instead of individuals. It is especially effective for people who respond well to tangible stimuli and are good at visual thinking. The steps are as follows:

❶ Each group receives a grocery sack containing various small items and toys such as little cars, funny glasses, balloons, corks, spinning tops, buttons, squirt guns, novelty items, and so forth. Novelty and toy stores are excellent sources for these items.

❷ One group member reaches into the bag without looking and retrieves an item.

❸ Group members describe the characteristics and traits of the item and use them to trigger ideas.

❹ Another group member selects a second item and the group uses it to suggest ideas.

❺ This process continues until the group has free-associated with all the items in the sack.

For an example of this process, see Tickler Things.

76. It's Not My Job

Have you ever been curious about other people's jobs? What exactly do they do? How do they do it? How do they feel about it? Henry Andersen (1991), a marketing manager for Mitsubishi Heavy Industries Europe, Ltd., had a similar curiosity. One difference was that his curiosity was directed more at how ideas could be generated by borrowing from different work disciplines.

Andersen developed "The Diamond Idea Group" to promote use of multidisciplinary perspectives during idea generation. He envisioned the Diamond Idea Group as a worldwide resource organizations could use to generate ideas for any number of problems. (For reasons outside his control, Andersen was not able to develop the Diamond Idea Group as he originally proposed. He now is working on a related concept.) His primary method for generating ideas is what he calls Trans-Disciplinary Analogy (TDA). According to Andersen, the steps for TDA are as follows:

❶ The leader divides people into small groups of at least five members each.

❷ The leader assigns a facilitator to each group.

❸ The facilitator asks each group member to select a discipline (professional or nonprofessional activity) of interest to that person. This discipline does not have to be that person's primary occupation or a traditional academic discipline. It may even be some activity such as gardening or building model airplanes. However, the group member should be knowledgeable about the discipline.

❹ Each group member selects a central concept or theme from his or her discipline. The facilitator records these concept on a notepad or flip chart.

❺ The group members select one of the concepts or themes and ask the contributor to describe it in some detail.

❻ Group members use the description to generate ideas.

❼ The group repeats steps 5 and 6 until enough ideas are generated.

Suppose the group want to improve a bathtub. One group member's interest area is gardening and his central concept is nurturing. The group selects this concept and the group member describes it as follows:

- ❢ Watering as needed

- ❢ Tilling to eliminate weeds

- ❢ Spraying insecticide to eliminate bugs

- Covering small plants during cold weather

- Adding fertilizer to promote growth

Next, the group uses these descriptions to suggest the following ideas:

- Button on top of tub (closer to hands) that adds more water when pushed

- Tub with built-in planter

- Tub that automatically sprays disinfectant inside tub after use

- Designer cover or cabinet to hide tub

- Tub that can be raised or lowered hydraulically to create a sunken tub look or to make it easier for older or disabled people to enter

77. Rolestorming

We all play various roles in our lives: butcher, baker, candlestick maker, mother, father, brother, teacher, friend, and so on. In one sense, we all are actors strutting on the stage of life (with apologies to the Bard). Life requires that we wear many different hats to interact with various people. We act our way through most interpersonal situations.

Most of our "acting" is genuine in that we aren't intentionally trying to become someone else. Rather, we may act out little scenarios to add spice to our interactions. Thus, we might sometimes put a little twist in our behavior and temporarily pretend we're someone else or act slightly out of character. Such role-playing behavior helps emphasize a point and simply makes life more interesting.

Role-playing also provides new perspectives. Marriage counselors often ask spouses to role-play a dialog from the other spouse's point of view. This allows both spouses to see things differently and increases their understanding of the other. As a result, they may think of new ways to interact.

Griggs (1985) invented the Rolestorming technique to capitalize on the advantages of role-playing. Griggs believes that many brainstorming sessions are unproductive because people feel inhibited. We take a risk every time we suggest something new. If our ideas are not received well, we stand to lose face.

To help prevent inhibition, Griggs suggests that group members generate ideas from someone else's perspective. He recommends the following steps:

❶ Group members defer judgment and generate twenty to thirty ideas, before the role-playing process.

❷ Each group member selects another person who is not present but is known to everyone present. This person could be a coworker, manager, secretary, staff person, or anyone else known to all group members.

❸ Individual group members think about the attitudes, preferences, opinions, and beliefs of the person they chose, and pretend that the person has a stake in the problem.

❹ Each group member generates ideas based on what he or she thinks this person might say. If any group members feel uncomfortable acting as their person, they might say instead, "My person would try to" or "My person would want to."

78. Roll Call

Are you an extrovert? Did you always try to answer teachers' questions in school? Do you like to shout out ideas when brainstorming? Do you shoot from the hip? If you answered yes to any of these questions, then you probably will like this booster.

Although we have been taught to think before we speak, this advice may sometimes be counterproductive. If we think too much before we talk during idea generation, we may judge our ideas prematurely and restrict our creativity. Self-censors are the enemies of all creative thought.

Unlike many situations in life, this booster works best when you talk before you think. Its major strength is that it encourages spontaneity and helps eliminate judgmental thinking. Group members are forced to leap to conclusions instead of leaping to ideas. Thus, they have little choice but to defer judgment. Hall (1994) describes the steps as follows:

❶ The group breaks up into smaller groups of four to six people.

❷ Three members of each group are selected to call out one word each. The words should be whatever pops into their heads. Group members shouldn't think very long about what word to say, and the words should be unrelated to the problem.

❸ All the group members then have 104 seconds to create a practical idea based on combining the three words or using the individual words for stimulation. (Hall doesn't say why he chose 104 seconds, but it really isn't important.)

❹ Repeat steps 2 and 3 until a sufficient number of ideas have been generated.

Here's a brief example to illustrate Roll Call using the problem of how to improve a kitchen table. Group members call out the words "radio," "penguin," and "icicle." The group then uses these words to prompt ideas:

- Radio built into the table

- Musical lazy Susan with a cooling mechanism that keeps food cold.

- Table designed with a tuxedo motif

- Table with holders to keep drinks cold

- Table with an "arctic" motif

- A penguin table with leaves that resemble penguin wings

79. Sculptures

For many people, a sculpture is a place for pigeons to light; for others, a sculpture may represent a sublime representation of the agonies of displaced human frailties (or some other equally esoteric line of art babble). However you perceive sculptures, they all represent different interpretations of reality. As such, they also are stimuli capable of prompting different perspectives.

If you've read much of this book, you probably have figured out that an ability to prompt different perspectives is a major characteristic of most brain boosters. An "aha!" should be going off in your head right now. Why not use sculptures to generate ideas?

Unfortunately, most people don't have ready access to sculptures. Although I might like to have a sculpture garden in my backyard, it will probably be a few years before that becomes a reality—if ever. Although most of us don't have the resources for our own sculpture collection, we could visit a local museum. But that's not always convenient or possible.

Another option is to create your own sculpture. Such a method has been used for years as a management training activity. I learned of this version while visiting a management consultant in Oslo, Norway. The consultant, Ole Faafeng (1986), devised this booster to help groups get more involved in brainstorming and to provide a source of unrelated stimuli. The steps are as follows:

❶ Each group starts with a variety of materials unrelated to the problem to be solved. For instance, groups might receive string, rope, blocks of wood, wire, books, colored paper, tape, scissors, paper clips, clay, cardboard, glue sticks, dowel rods, crayons, small chairs, and rubber balls.

❷ Each group looks over the materials and constructs a sculpture that represents an abstract version of the problem (or the group may construct a sculpture completely unrelated to the problem).

❸ When done, group members then discuss their sculpture and note structures, parts, and relationships.

❹ The group uses its sculpture as a source of stimulation and begins generating ideas.

Faafeng describes how one group used Sculptures to improve communication within an organization. Part of the sculpture involved a string stretched between two objects. The string reminded one group member of a communication network within the organization. He then thought of a way to alter a communication line in a novel way. Other group members joined in and refined and elaborated on his idea.

80. Super Heroes

"Look! Up in the sky! It's a bird! It's a plane!" These words, which describe the super hero Superman, may evoke childhood memories of super deeds and exploits—days when a fantasy character could come to our rescue. Then we grew up and learned that our super heroes are imaginary and may not always be there for us. Well, fret not. The Super Heroes have returned! And now they can help us solve some real-world problems.

Consultants Grossman and Catlin (1985) developed Super Heroes as a way to introduce a playful spirit during brainstorming sessions. (See VanGundy, 1988 for a more detailed description.) Group members assume the identity of various super heroes and use the characters' perspectives to prompt ideas. The steps are as follows:

❶ Group members review a set of descriptions of super heroes.

❷ Each group member selects a character and assumes that character's identity. If group members really want to get into the spirit, they may don their characters' costumes; if not, each group member wears a sign around his or her neck with the name of the character on it.

❸ Individual group members read their character descriptions silently. They then summarize these descriptions aloud, describing special powers, strengths, weaknesses, habits, and other special characteristics.

❹ After hearing each character description, all the group members use the descriptions as stimuli for ideas. For instance, Superman's x-ray vision might suggest using hidden camaras to detect employee and customer theft in a store.

Here are some sample super heroes and their major characteristics:

- Batman—first-rate detective; can outwit the worst criminals; uses bat paraphernalia such as a Batmobile, a Batplane, a Batcycle, Batrollerskates, and a Batrope. Batman's alter ego is millionaire Bruce Wayne.

- Captain America—represents the ultimate in American ideals (truth, justice, mom, apple pie), has a winning personality with great powers of persuasion, maintains a positive outlook on life, is very athletic, and uses his Captain America Shield to protect himself from harm.

- Dr. Strange—a skilled magician and sorcerer who can create numerous illusions. He can also cure sicknesses, control people and situations, and transform objects into other objects. He often has temporary losses of concentration.

- Mr. Fantastic—the smartest man in the world; can stretch his body into any length and has tremendous flexibility.

- The Human Torch—a short-tempered hothead who has the power to emit and control fire without burning himself. He also can fly.

- The Invisible Girl—can make herself or other people and things invisible and make them reappear. When in danger, she creates an invisible shield that protects her from harm.

- Superman—has x-ray vision and super hearing, can fly faster than a speeding bullet, and is the strongest man on earth. Clark Kent, mild-mannered newspaper reporter, is his alter ego. Can be weakened only by Kryptonite. Is able to leap tall buildings in a single bound. Often mistaken for birds or airplanes.

- Wonder Woman—a truly liberated woman with super strength, agility, and athletic ability who can overpower anyone. Has magical bracelets that deflect bullets, and she can capture almost anything or anyone with her magical lasso. Once lassoed by Wonder Woman, a person must tell the truth. Flies an invisible airplane.

BRAIN BOOSTERS FOR BUSINESS ADVANTAGE

11

Brainwriting With Related Boosters

The group boosters in this chapter produce ideas using silent idea generation with stimuli related to the problem. These boosters may not produce ideas as unique as ideas generated using unrelated boosters. However, the right combination of group members can spark ideas regardless of the techniques used.

As with other brainwriting methods, some boosters in this chapter require group members to share their ideas, whereas others involve no sharing. (Boosters in this chapter that don't involve sharing during the idea generation process include Group Not [83], Organizational Brainstorms [87], and Your Slip Is Showing [90].) Research suggests that sharing should produce more ideas and higher-quality ideas.

Brainwriting, with or without sharing, may be one of the best ways to guarantee large numbers of ideas in a group. When compared to conventional brainstorming techniques, the Brain Purge booster [82] described in this chapter has been found to be especially useful for increasing idea quantity in groups. Recent research by Van-Gundy has shown that Brain Purge groups generate four times as many ideas as conventional brainstorming groups. And, as you know, idea quantity is often linked to idea quality.

So what makes brainwriting so special? Brainwriting boosters compensate for a serious deficiency of most brainstorming groups. Specifically, only one person can generate ideas at a time during brainstorming. This is known as "production blocking." Brainwriting overcomes production blocking by enabling all group members to generate ideas at the same time.

Most brainwriting boosters also are simple and easy to use. What more could you want in a group technique? After all, the objective of most idea generation sessions is to think of lots of ideas.

Unfortunately, the downside of brainwriting is that most people enjoy the social satisfaction that accompanies brainstorming. In brainstorming groups, productivity often takes a back seat to satisfaction of social needs. So what to do? Use both brainstorming and brainwriting. They complement each other nicely.

81. As Easy As 6-3-5

As Easy As 6-3-5, originally known as Method 6-3-5 (VanGundy, 1988), is a very basic brain-writing procedure that structures how people interact and generate ideas. There are at least three versions of this booster, so you get three boosters in one. Here they are:

Version 1

John Warfield and his colleagues (1975) developed the first version of this booster:

❶ Six people sit around a table and discuss the problem.

❷ Each group member writes down three ideas in a five-minute period.

❸ At the end of the five minutes, group members pass their papers to the person on their right.

❹ The person receiving a paper examines the ideas and tries to generate new ideas or elaborations.

❺ This process continues until each group member receives his or her original paper.

Version 2

German creativity consultant Horst Geschka and associates (1981) developed the second version of this booster. Some claim it is the first brain-writing method. The steps are as follows:

❶ Six people are seated around a table. Each receives a sheet of paper containing three columns, with one idea listed at the top of each column.

❷ Group members write down at least one idea that improves on the one listed at the top of the column. (If no improvements are generated, participants write down new ideas.)

❸ After five minutes, group members pass their papers to the person on their right and the process continues until all members receive their original papers.

Version 3

The third version described here was originated by creativity consultants in Germany and Holland and was further developed by University of Manchester business professor Tudor Rickards (1974). It is similar to the other versions except that it is slightly more structured and no time limit is imposed. Here are the steps:

❶ Six people are seated around a table. Each group member receives three cards and writes the problem on each one.

❷ Group members write one idea on each card and pass their cards to another, pre-

BRAIN BOOSTERS FOR BUSINESS ADVANTAGE

selected member (for example, member 1 may be instructed to pass the cards to member 4).

❸ Members receiving the cards read them and write any new ideas or improvements on the cards.

❹ Group members pass their cards to the next designated person and the process continues until group members have responded to each idea five times.

82. Brain Purge

Before we can think of creative solutions, we often must purge ourselves of more traditional or obvious ideas. Brain Purge, originally developed by Geschka (1979) as Pin Cards, allows you to flush out ideas you can think of immediately or ideas you have been waiting to express. However, don't use this booster just to get rid of conventional ideas. It also is a handy way to generate many ideas—in a relatively short time—for almost any problem situation. You'll find that Brain Purge is similar to As Easy As 6-3-5 [81], but not as structured.

The steps are as follows:

❶ Each member of a five-person group has a stack of index cards (or Post-it Notes).

❷ Participants write one idea on a card and pass it to the person on their right.

❸ Group members read the ideas on the cards they just received and use these ideas to stimulate improvements or entirely new ideas.

❹ Group members write any improvements or new ideas on new cards and pass them to the person on their right.

❺ This process continues for about ten to fifteen minutes. Time is called and the cards are collected and sorted into categories for evaluation. The cards may then be pinned to a bulletin board for review (or Post-it Notes may be put on a wall).

83. Group Not

The title of this booster refers to an interesting question in small-group problem solving: When is a group not a group? The answer is that a group isn't a group when members don't interact during group activity. Such nongroups are known as "nominal" groups.

Group Not is based on what probably is the most heavily researched small-group idea generation technique: the Nominal Group Technique (NGT). NGT was developed by Delbecq and Van de Ven (1971). Although this method allows group members to discuss their ideas, the members do so only after all the ideas have been generated.

As with similar boosters, a major disadvantage of NGT is that group members don't see each other's ideas during idea generation. On the other hand, this technique provides a highly structured process for both idea generation and evaluation. There are six steps:

❶ *Silent Generation of Ideas in Writing.* Five people in a group individually write down ideas without sharing them with others.

❷ *Round Robin Recording of Ideas.* Group members take turns reading aloud one of their ideas, and the leader records and numbers these ideas on a flip chart. During this activity, no ideas are discussed.

❸ *Serial Discussion for Clarification.* The leader points to each idea and asks for discussion. The purpose of this activity is to clarify the meaning, purpose, or logic behind each idea.

❹ *Preliminary Vote on Item Importance.* Group members select between five and nine favorite ideas and write each on a separate card. Members write the number of the idea (from the master list) in the upper left corner of each card and record their rating of the idea (1 = not important; 5 = important) in the lower left corner. The leader collects all the cards and records the votes on a flip chart. Finally, the leader notes the idea receiving the greatest number

of votes. If a clear winner emerges, the process ends.

❺ *Discussion of the Preliminary Vote.* If no clear winner emerges or there is some doubt about the vote tallies, group members examine the vote tally sheets for peculiar patterns (for example, if an idea receives many high and low votes). If they notice an odd pattern, group members discuss the item to clarify why that pattern resulted.

❻ *Final Vote.* If necessary, a final vote is taken using the procedure described for the preliminary vote. This step provides group members with a sense of closure.

84. Idea Mixer

I don't know much Japanese, so I have to assume that Hiroshi Takahashi is correct when he says that NHK is a Japanese acronym for the Japan Broadcasting Corporation. Takahashi developed what I call Idea Mixer while working for NHK (he calls the method NHK Brainstorming). Although he refers to it as a brainstorming technique and it involves some oral idea generation, Idea Mixer actually is a combination brainwriting/brainstorming booster. The steps are as follows:

❶ Individuals receive five index cards and write one idea on each card.

❷ The participants form groups of five.

❸ As each individual discusses his or her idea, other group members write down new ideas that come to mind.

❹ The cards are collected and grouped into categories of related themes.

❺ Participants form new groups of two or three people, brainstorm ideas for the themes, and write the ideas on index cards.

❻ After one hour, each group sorts its ideas by themes and presents these ideas to the larger group. The ideas are written where they will be visible to all.

❼ Participants form new groups of ten people and brainstorm ways to improve the ideas listed.

85. Idea Pool

Idea Pool (also known as Brainwriting Pool) is a close relative of the Brain Purge method [82]. It was developed at the Battelle Institute in Frankfurt, Germany (Geschka, Schaude, and Schlicksupp, 1973). One difference between the two boosters is in how the

ideas are shared among the group members. In Brain Purge, members pass ideas around the group, whereas in Idea Pool members put ideas in the center of a table to form a "pool." The steps are as follows:

❶ Five people are seated around a table, and each person silently writes four ideas on a sheet of paper.

❷ Each group member places the sheet of paper in the center of the table and exchanges it for another sheet.

❸ Participants examine the ideas on the new sheet and write down improvements or new ideas. They then place this sheet in the center of the table and exchange it for a new one.

❹ After ten to fifteen minutes of this activity, the idea sheets are collected, and the ideas are later evaluated.

86. Museum Madness

Museum Madness (also known as the Gallery Method) is another of the many group boosters originally developed at the Battelle Institute in Frankfurt, Germany, by Horst Geschka and his associates (1981). It is similar to other group boosters that use unrelated stimuli. However, it is different in one significant way: instead of passing ideas around the group, members walk around to the ideas. Thus, Museum Madness reverses the process that most group brainwriting methods use. The title of the booster derives from the way people browse around a museum looking at works of art. The steps are quite simple:

❶ The leader attaches sheets of flip-chart paper to the walls of a room (flip charts on stands may also be used).

❷ Each group member silently writes ideas on one sheet of paper.

❸ After about fifteen to twenty minutes of writing, the participants spend fifteen minutes walking around the room, reading the other ideas, and taking notes.

❹ Group members again silently generate ideas on one sheet of flip-chart paper. This time they try to use the other ideas to stimulate improvements or new ideas.

❺ At the end of the second round of idea generation, the group evaluates all the ideas.

87. Organizational Brainstorms

John Haefele (1961), an employee of Procter & Gamble, developed this booster more than thirty years ago and called it the Collective Notebook Method. It is unique among group boosters in that it is the only method in which ideas are not generated in a small-group setting. Instead, ideas come from a select group of employees through-out an organization.

The original version of Organizational Brain-storms is somewhat similar to Group Not [83] and Your Slip Is Showing [90]. All these boosters involve generating ideas without sharing them with other participants. A revised version, how-ever, does permit limited idea sharing. The steps for the original version are as follows:

❶ Preselected participants from throughout an organization (representing different ar-eas of knowledge related to the problem) each receive a notebook containing prob-lem information and instructions on the process.

❷ Each participant writes one idea per day in the notebook.

❸ At the end of one month, the participants summarize their best ideas.

❹ The coordinator collects all the notebooks, records and categorizes the ideas, and pre-pares a summary.

❺ The participants are given access to the summary and may be invited to discuss the ideas generated.

Alan Pearson (1979) has used this booster with one significant variation: Participants proceed as just described, except they exchange their note-books with another person after two weeks. Par-ticipants then use the ideas in the new notebooks to trigger additional ideas over the remaining two weeks.

88. Out-of-the-Blue Lightening Bolt Cloudbuster

Hall (1994) developed this booster to spark ideas during extended group idea generation sessions. As with some other boosters in this chapter, written ideas are shared among group members. However, the procedure used to share ideas is much more unstructured (to say the least): Group members write their ideas on paper airplanes and throw them about. The result can be a lot of fun. And where there's fun, there are often many creative ideas. Here's how to use this booster:

❶ Each group member receives a plentiful supply of conventional paper airplanes (at least ten planes per participant).

❷ During an extended idea generation session, the participants are told that whenever they think of an idea, they should write it on the wings of an airplane and throw the plane into a designated location (for example, a nonburning fireplace, a box, or a corner of the room).

❸ At the end of the idea session, the airplanes are distributed to the group members, and participants fly the planes to someone else.

❹ Participants examine the idea written on the airplane, write down any improvements or new ideas, and then launch the airplane again. Participants should write whatever comes to mind. This process is repeated until each plane has flown four or five times.

❺ All the airplanes are collected, and the group evaluates the ideas.

89. You're a Card, Andy!

Many people play cards to relax and enjoy the company of others. Others play cards to escape their troubles. For instance, I remember fellow students in college who loved to play cards. Unfortunately, many of them loved playing cards more than they loved studying. After less than a year, most of these folks found that they had all the time in the world to play cards—no college education, but plenty of time for cards.

One conclusion from this story may be that playing cards can be unproductive. This is true if card playing is taken to extremes. It is possible, however, to play cards while generating ideas. Thus, you can have fun while also being productive. (Where are you now, college friends? I may have a job for you.)

You're a Card, Andy! is a brainwriting method developed by Goodman and Shields (1993). It is similar to Brain Purge [82] but has the potential to generate a more fun atmosphere. Just be careful that the group doesn't pay more attention to playing cards than to generating ideas. Here are the steps (slightly modified):

❶ Group members receive seven index cards as their "starting hand."

❷ Group members write one idea on a card and deal it to anyone they choose in the group.The only restriction is that each member must receive at least two cards. They continue this process for a specified time period (for example, five minutes) or until there is a lull in activity.

❸ Each member shows his or her "hand," and the group creates a "pot" of additional ideas. Each person is asked to ante up in turn.

❹ The last person with an additional idea wins a dream date, vacation, or whatever prize the group decides is appropriate.

❺ Group members pin the cards to a wall or lay them out on a table in logical clusters.

❻ Group members review the ideas and see if any new ideas are prompted. If so, they add new idea cards to the clusters.

90. Your Slip Is Showing

This booster (also known as Crawford Slipwriting) may be the "mother of all brain boosters"—at least in terms of being a progenitor of brainwriting methods. Dr. C. C. Crawford developed this technique in the United States in the 1920s (see Whiting, 1958; Crawford and Demidovitch, 1983), and Charles Clark (1978) has popularized the method over the past thirty or so years. It is especially useful when you want to gather ideas from a large number of people. According to Clark, the steps are as follows:

❶ Each person (in a group of up to five thousand) receives a pad or stack of paper slips measuring roughly three by five inches.

❷ Participants begin writing one idea on each slip of paper.

❸ After five to ten minutes, the participants stop writing and the group leader collects the slips.

❹ The leader appoints a task force to evaluate the ideas. This task force first sorts the ideas into categories according to frequency of occurrence or degree of usability. Then the task force selects the best ideas and develops them into workable proposals.

Clark also suggests some variations, such as using abstract graphics to prompt ideas. Or participants could divide into pairs and one person in the pair could record ideas for both people— a sort of mini-brainstorming group.

CHAPTER
12

Brainwriting With Unrelated Boosters

The brain boosters in Chapter 11 are all based on stimuli related to the problem. Theoretically this means that the resulting ideas may not be as unique as those generated with unrelated stimuli. Of course, that's not always the case, because other factors (such as a highly creative personality) may determine the quality of a group's ideas. All things being equal, however, unrelated stimuli are more likely to lead to winning ideas.

The boosters in this chapter are based on sources of stimulation not related directly to the problem. In that respect, they resemble the unrelated brainstorming boosters in Chapter 10. The difference, of course, is that the boosters in this chapter are based on basic brainwriting techniques (the silent, written generation of ideas in a group).

Some research suggests that brainwriting techniques—regardless of the stimulus source—may outperform brainstorming methods. Thus, unrelated brainwriting boosters have the highest theoretical potential to produce hot ideas. Note that the operative word is "theoretical." The best boosters for you may represent all categories. You'll just have to experiment and see which ones work best.

91. Altered States

Many of the boosters are based on changing perspectives. Creating a new way of seeing things disrupts locked-in viewpoints. Although many people fear change, changing perspectives should be welcomed in creative thinking. Altering a dysfunctional or narrow perspective can provide the insights needed to generate breakthrough ideas. Change your perspective and you'll open up new worlds of thought.

Hall (1994) developed Altered States to help people change their frames of reference and see their problems differently. Once a person's perspective has changed, new ideas should flow more freely. Here are the steps for this booster:

❶ Each group member uses the following questions and lists three bizarre, wild altered states for the problem. Don't over analyze or be too concerned with practicality. Just be spontaneous.

- When is the product or service consumed or purchased?

  Response 1: _____

  Response 2: _____

  Response 3: _____

- Why is the product or service consumed or purchased?

  Response 1: _____

  Response 2: _____

  Response 3: _____

- Where is the product or service consumed or purchased?

  Response 1: _____

  Response 2: _____

  Response 3: _____

- What components, ingredients, or elements make up the product or service?

  Response 1: _____

  Response 2: _____

  Response 3: _____

❷ Group members pass their lists to another group member.

❸ Group members examine the lists they receive and use the responses to trigger ideas.

As an example, suppose you want to generate cereal product and marketing ideas. First, list bizarre, wild altered states:

- 💡 When is the product or service consumed or purchased?

  Response 1: In the bathtub

  Response 2: When the user craves vampire blood

  Response 3: When the user is rolling on the floor

- 💡 Why is the product or service consumed or purchased?

  Response 1: To alleviate boredom

  Response 2: To cure cancer

  Response 3: To impress the neighbors

- 💡 Where is the product or service consumed or purchased?

  Response 1: In Martian vending machines

  Response 2: In public restrooms

  Response 3: In butcher shops

- What components, ingredients, or elements make up the product or service?

  Response 1: Silly Putty

  Response 2: Light bulbs

  Response 3: Bricks

If you received this list of responses, it might help you think of such ideas as

- Cereal boxes shaped like bathtubs

- Cereal shaped like blood clots to "gross out" children

- Designer cereal boxes with snob appeal

- Cereal sold in vending machines

- Meat-flavored cereal that doubles as pet food

- Transparent cereal boxes

- Cereal boxes that, when empty, can be used as molds for bricks to build homes for the homeless

92. Balloon, Balloon, Balloon

The fun factor is an important ingredient during any idea generation session. Several boosters in this book incorporate fun elements to heighten creative perceptions and increase the potential for large numbers of ideas, and Balloon, Balloon,

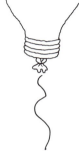

Balloon is one of them. Although this booster is similar to others, the built-in fun factor can provide the lift a group needs to generate hot ideas. Try it right after lunch and I guarantee no one will fall asleep. According to its developer, Hall (1994), the steps are as follows:

❶ The group leader obtains a supply of balloons—at least four for each group, although more will probably be better. The balloons should be at least twelve inches in diameter and come in two colors (half in one color and half in the other color.

❷ The leader prepares two sets of paper slips, small enough to be inserted into the balloons. Group members write one silly, abstract, nonsensical phrase on each slip from the first set (for example, "rhubarb ink javelins," "worm lips on parade," "rotating cat lemons", "vibrating elephants in your ear.") On each slip from the second set, they write one word or phrase related to the problem.

❸ Members insert one silly-word slip into each balloon of one color and insert a related-problem-word slip into each balloon of the other color.

❹ The group leader turns on music, and the members of all groups tap the balloons back and forth (if there is only one group, the individual members bat the balloons around.)

❺ When the music stops (or time is called), groups collect the balloons next to them. Each group should try to gather at least one balloon of each color. Team members then sit on their balloons to pop them.

❻ Groups combine ideas from one balloon of each color and use the combination as a stimulus for new ideas. They repeat this process until they have considered all possible pairs of ideas.

As an example, suppose you want ideas about how to sell more office chairs. Your group examines several slips from the balloons and comes up with the following ideas:

- Pen holders built into a chair's arms (from "arms" and "rhubarb ink javelins")

- A self-propelled office chair (from "wheels" and "rhubarb ink javelins")

- A chair with a drink holder for different cup sizes (from "arms" and "rotating cat lemons")

- A built-in vibrating seat and back (from "back" and "vibrating elephants in your ear")

- A built-in stereo radio in the top of the seat back (from "back" and "vibrating elephants in your ear")

93. Bouncing Ball

You've probably heard the expression "Let's bounce that idea around." Well, this booster allows a group to do almost exactly that. Bouncing Ball is a fun booster, and it's probably one of the easiest boosters to implement as well. The steps are as follows:

❶ The group leader obtains two or three foam Nerf balls about four inches in diameter.

❷ Group members throw the balls around for a few minutes. Then the leader collects all the balls except one.

❸ Whoever is holding the ball throws it to another group member. Whoever catches the ball shouts out a random word or phrase. This person then throws the ball to another person, who shouts out a word related to the problem.

❹ Someone writes down these two words as a combination, and the entire group uses the combination to stimulate new ideas.

❺ After all ideas are exhausted for that combination, the last person to catch the ball throws it to someone else, and steps 3 and 4 are repeated.

The basic elements of Bouncing Ball are virtually identical to those of Balloon, Balloon, Balloon [92]. A major difference is in how the random and nonrandom words are selected. Bouncing Ball is easier to implement, but Balloon, Balloon, Balloon will probably provide more sustained fun.

94. Brainsketching

If you're like many people, you may enjoy drawing doodles and sketches of various objects. You may do this absentmindedly while talking on the phone, for instance, or intentionally while trying to visualize some problem aspect.

Brainsketching draws on this natural activity and applies it in a group setting.

Brainsketching was developed by Pickens (1980) as a modification of the Brain Purge booster [82]. The primary difference is that Brainsketching involves passing pictures around a group instead of ideas. Another distinction is that the sketches may be more abstract and symbolic than the ideas used by the Brain Purge method. The steps are as follows:

❶ Each group member draws a sketch of a problem solution. This sketch doesn't need to represent a direct, clear-cut solution; it may be relatively abstract and symbolic. No talking is permitted while sketching, and the sketches should not be shared.

❷ After five minutes, group members pass their sketches to the person on their right.

❸ Group members receiving a sketch review it and try to improve it by adding to the sketch, making brief comments, or drawing an entirely new sketch. They then pass this drawing to the person on their right.

❹ Group members repeat steps one through three until time is called.

❺ All the sketches are collected and reviewed, and any new ideas stimulated by the sketches are recorded.

95. Doodlin' Around the Block Game

This Brain Booster is a little like Brainsketching in that it involves some doodling. Brainsketching uses doodles of pictures and abstract symbols; Doodlin' Around the Block Game, in contrast, uses a very specific type of doodle: a square or rectangle. It also differs in that it is a game which introduces some competition, much like the Name Game described elsewhere in this chapter.

Assume that you manufacture food products and decide to generate some snack food ideas. You assemble a group of six people who agree to play Doodlin' Around the Block. The steps are as follows:

 A small group sits around a sheet of flip chart paper on a table or on the floor.

 Each group member writes on the paper one word unrelated to the problem. The words are written approximately the same distance from each other and spread out around the paper. Group members use the unrelated words as stimuli to trigger ideas. An example is shown below in which the six group members have written down six different unrelated words.

---

fires   lamps

                              cannons   fish

ball   paper

 Individuals begin drawing squares from the edges of the paper and write ideas inside them, one idea per box. They can draw squares in any direction as long as they are connected. However, members must draw each square—about two inches by two inches—without lifting up their pens or pencils. Thus, each square will be connected. Group members who no longer can connect squares must stop writing. As they draw boxes, they write down any ideas they can think of inside the boxes. An example of the idea boxes follows.

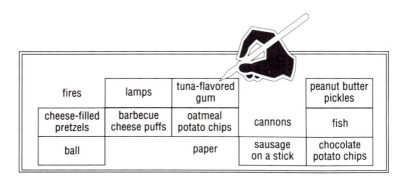

fires	lamps	tuna-flavored gum		peanut butter pickles
cheese-filled pretzels	barbecue cheese puffs	oatmeal potato chips	cannons	fish
ball		paper	sausage on a stick	chocolate potato chips

❹ One point is given for each idea in every box. Whoever draws a box around one of the unrelated words wins two bonus points for each word. The person with the most points is declared the winner.

In the example, boxes have been drawn around three of the unrelated stimulus words and seven snack food product ideas for a total of 10 boxes. The 10 boxes mean that at least 10 total points will be awarded. Because three of the boxes contain unrelated words, six bonus points will be awarded for grand total of 16 points.

96. Greeting Cards

There is little doubt that a playful group atmosphere is more likely to result in quality ideas than a more staid, serious environment. Several research studies have found that humor and creativity go hand in hand. When laughter is present, good ideas seem to appear.

Many of the brain boosters in this book help create a fun environment. Prominent among these are Spin the Bottle [67]; Battle of the Sexes [71]; Sculptures [79]; Super Heroes [80]; and Balloon, Balloon, Balloon [92]. In addition, the Greeting Cards booster seems to work especially well for making creative thinking fun.

Greeting Cards is a hands-on technique that allows group members to express themselves in an environment conducive to creative thinking. Unlike most boosters, the group leader should avoid telling the group the problem if possible (the problem will be revealed later as part of the process). According to the method's developer, Pickens (1985), the steps are as follows:

❶ Each group receives the materials needed to create greeting cards, including such items as magazines and catalogs (for pictures), scissors, colored construction paper, glue sticks, markers, crayons, pens, and adhesive tape.

❷ Group members look through the catalogs and magazines and cut out about ten pictures that look interesting.

❸ Group members paste the pictures onto folded sheets of paper and write catchy text. The most effective cards use humor for traditional themes such as belated birthday, divorce, friendship, or get well.

❹ After all the cards are constructed, group members are told the problem.

❺ Group members use the text, pictures, and themes of the cards as stimuli for ideas.

❻ If there is more than one group, groups may exchange cards and use them to trigger additional ideas.

VanGundy (1988) used Greeting Cards to help an airline generate ideas to attract international passengers. One of the groups created a card for a recently divorced male friend. The front of the card read "True, the judge may have awarded her the alimony..." When the card was opened, a picture of a male torso in underwear was revealed. The caption under this picture read "...So we're awarding you support." Group members used this card to think of designing seats with adjustable support (such as an inflatable lumbar support).

97. The Name Game

In developing the Name Game (also known as the Brainwriting Game), Woods (1979), sought to create a technique that was fun but did not require a high degree of leader or participant skills. This booster also provides competition to motivate group members.

Another advantage of The Name Game is that it uses impractical ideas as a source for practical solutions. Improbable ideas (which are also used as the basis for the Get Real!! booster [60]) have great potential to trigger workable ideas.

Although this booster is slightly more complex than other brainwriting methods, it still is easy to implement. The steps are as follows:

❶ Group members are told that the objective of the exercise is to develop the most improbable idea. Whoever suggests the least probable idea wins the game.

❷ Each group member buys numbered, but otherwise blank, cards from a facilitator at one cent each.

❸ On each card purchased, participants write the most improbable idea they can imagine.

❹ All ideas are displayed for the entire group to read.

❺ Individuals study each idea and try to think of ways to make it more practical to reduce the idea owner's chances of winning. Group members may not talk during this activity.

❻ After about twenty minutes, group members are asked to cast votes for the two most improbable ideas. The person whose idea receives the most votes is awarded the money that was exchanged for the cards.

❼ The group divides into two subgroups, and each subgroup is given one-half of the cards.

❽ Groups use the ideas on the cards to stimulate a minimum of six practical problem solutions.

❾ After twenty minutes, each group tries to "sell" its ideas to the other group. Both groups then try to agree on a final list of the best ideas.

98. Pass the Buck

"Passing the buck" is an old expression meaning avoiding responsibility by blaming or otherwise involving someone else. Various take-charge presidents and business executives helped popularize the expression by asserting that "the buck stops here." Hall (1994) has created a new use for the phrase "pass the buck" by developing a brain booster using the expression.

Pass the Buck was designed to be used by four different small groups. It can be easily modified, however, for just one group. The steps for four groups are as follows:

❶ Each group receives one copy of a Pass the Buck worksheet (Figure 12-1).

❷ The leader plays loud music while each group generates an "Absurd, Bizarre, Exotic Idea" and writes it in cell 1 on the worksheet.

❸ Each group passes its worksheet to another group.

❹ The groups examine the first idea, write a "Somewhat Realistic" version of this idea in cell 2, and pass this worksheet to another group.

❺ The groups examine the worksheet passed to them, write an idea that is "A Little More Realistic" in cell 3, and pass this worksheet to another group. The groups then write down the final, most realistic idea in cell 4, which is entitled "The Buck Stops Here."

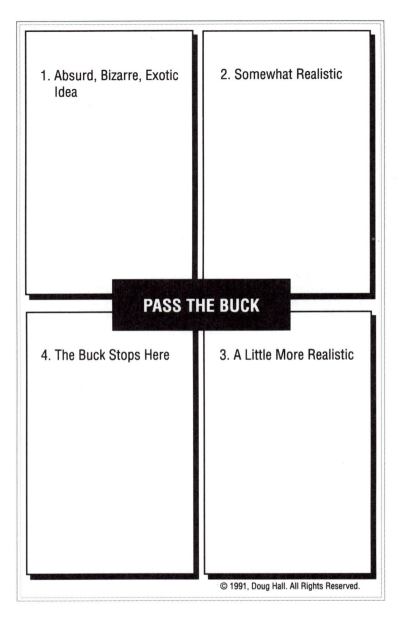

Figure 12-1. Pass the Buck

BRAIN BOOSTERS FOR BUSINESS ADVANTAGE

❻ The groups share all their ideas with the other groups, and any new ideas are recorded.

If you have just one group, you can modify this booster easily, especially if you have only four group members. Just have one group member write an idea in each of the cells. If you have more than four members, have them double up to fill in the cells.

99. Post It, Pardner!

You agreed to send Fred in Accounting a report. You don't want to, but you've got to. It's a real pain. You've got so many other important things to do, such as deciding where to eat lunch.

Time is running out. It's almost lunchtime and you promised Fred you would get him the report right after lunch. The problem is that you need to explain some minor details. You don't feel like firing up the computer and typing an official memo.

"Wait a minute," you mumble to yourself. "I'll just attach a Post-it Note and not bother with an official memo. Then I can get to lunch sooner." So you rip off a Post-it Note and scribble a brief message on it.

Those semisticky Post-it Notes are good for something besides avoiding typing memos. They can also help you generate ideas in a group and have fun as well. You'll need one pad of three-by-five inch Post-it Notes, a group, and a meeting room. That's it. This is a minimalist brain booster.

Post It, Pardner! is a relative of Museum Madness [86], in which group members write ideas on flip-chart sheets attached to a wall and then browse around the room using others' ideas as stimuli for new ideas. Post It, Pardner! uses a similar process, except this booster relies on unrelated stimuli to help trigger ideas. Specifically, instead of using ideas to prompt new ideas, group members use free associations generated by other group members. Here's how it works:

Each group member

❶ Receives three Post-it Notes

❷ Selects an object in the room (such as a lamp, window, door, table, chair, or coffee-pot) and uses the object as the stimulus for free associations

❸ Writes one free association on each note and sticks the note on or near the object

❹ Examines the free associations written by other group members and uses them to spark new ideas

❺ Writes the new ideas on new Post-it Notes

To illustrate, suppose your group wants to generate ways to improve a bed. Group members place Post-it Notes on the following objects and write the following associations:

● Door: wood, grain, alcohol

- Window: glass, clear, seeing

- Table: flat, smooth, slippery

- Coffeepot: hot, cold, icy

- Lamp: light, dark, black

The group then generates ideas using these associations:

- A built-in cereal dispenser (from "grain")

- An alcoholic beverage dispenser (from "alcohol")

- A bed with a slide on the bottom (from "slippery")

- A built-in heating and cooling apparatus (from "hot" and "cold")

- A built-in ice machine (from "icy")

- Variable lighting brightness and focus (from "light" and "dark")

100. Puzzle Pieces

In some respects, most problems are like jigsaw puzzles. We have to look over all the pieces, keep the big picture in mind, identify the boundaries, and plunge in and begin problem solving. If everything works out, we'll solve the puzzle and go on to other things. The Puzzle Pieces booster takes advantage

of these similarities by using pieces of a jigsaw
puzzle to put together ideas. Here's how it works:

❶ The group leader buys a small jigsaw puzzle with blank pieces (such puzzles are
available from educational supply companies and a few mail-order catalogs such as
Lillian Vernon). If a blank puzzle isn't available, the group can use the back side of a
standard puzzle.

❷ The leader mixes up the puzzle pieces and
divides them equally among the group
members.

❸ Each group member writes one practical
idea on the first piece, an unrelated word
on the second piece, a practical idea on the
third piece, an unrelated word on the fourth
piece, and so on until all the pieces have
been used.

❹ The group members attempt to assemble
the puzzle. After they have finished, they
select two adjacent pieces and use the
combination to spark ideas. They write
down the ideas, select another two adjacent pieces, and continue this process until
time is called.

101. The Shirt Off Your Back

If you're a manager of a business, there are times
when you would give the "shirt off your back" for
a hot new idea. Well, this booster may help you

get the idea you need, and you can keep your shirt on. Here's what to do:

❶ The group leader draws a picture of a shirt and makes a photocopy for each group member, or orders a box of paper with a shirt design (for example, The Paper Direct Company [1-800-A-PAPERS] sells paper with a full-page shirt graphic).

❷ The group divides into two subgroups out of hearing range of each other. The first subgroup is told to generate ideas for the true problem; the second subgroup is told to generate ideas for a completely unrelated problem.

❸ The subgroups reunite and each group member receives a piece of masking tape (about four inches long) to attach to the top of his or her "shirt sheet."

❹ Each group member writes on the shirt sheet one idea for resolving the assigned problem (that is, members of one subgroup write ideas for the true problem, while members of the other subgroup write ideas for an unrelated problem). Each participant then attaches the sheet to someone's back using the masking tape.

❺ Group members walk around the room reading the ideas on each other's backs and use these ideas as stimuli to generate new ideas. When group members think of an idea, they write it on the paper attached to the other person's back.

❻ After about ten to fifteen minutes of this activity, all the idea shirt sheets are collected and spread out on a large table or taped to a wall.

❼ Group members read aloud all the ideas, including those unrelated to the true problem, and try to generate a new idea from each one.

APPENDIX

Brain Booster Tools

The Brain Boosters in this book represent basic and often exotic procedures for producing a large number of ideas. You really can't go wrong using any of the boosters. There may be times, however, when you want a little variety. Or you may want to experiment with different idea generation tools—tangible aids for sparking ideas in individuals and groups. A number of idea generation tools exist and complement the brain boosters in this book. Two categories of tools are presented here: (1) traditional, "hands-on" idea stimulation tools, and (2) creativity software programs. Prices and vendor information are given. Please note that this information is subject to change.

Hands-on Tools

Circles of Creativity

The Circles of Creativity consist of an approximately 10-inch square with a rotating disk riveted in the center. Spinning the disk helps the user select roughly 170 word stimuli organized into four categories: "Try to..." and "Make it..." (selected with an arrow) and "Think About..." and "Add or Take Away..." (selected with cutouts). Featured in *U.S. News & World Report* and *Success* magazines.

VanGundy & Associates
1700 Winding Ridge Road
Norman, OK 73072
405-321-1309
Price: $15 with quantity discounts available

Creative Whack Pack

This is a deck of 64 idea-stimulating cards based on Roger van Oech's book, *A Whack on the Side of the Head*. The cards list quotes, motivational phrases, and suggestions for thinking of new ideas.

Creative Think
Menlo Park, CA
Price: $13.95

The Pocket Innovator

The Pocket Innovator presents idea stimuli on 150 1" x 4.5" plastic cards held together on one end by a rivet, much like a deck of paint chips. Key words, much like those on the Circles of Creativity and the Productive Improvement CheckList, stimulate ideas within a seven-step problem-solving process.

Creative Learning International
118 N. Clinton, Suite 207
Chicago, IL 60661
312-853-4748
Price: $49.50

Product Improvement CheckList (PICL)

PICL is an expanded, two-sided poster version (20" x 26") of the Circles of Creativity. It contains almost 600 idea stimulators, however, arranged in the same four categories: "Try to..." "Make it..." "Think About..." "Take Away or Add." Instead of spinning a wheel, users select words at random by pointing, dropping a coin, or throwing a dart (not included).

VanGundy & Associates
1700 Winding Ridge Road
Norman, OK 73072
405-321-1309
Price: $10 with quantity discounts available

Creativity Software

Idea Fisher

Idea Fisher helps generate ideas by enhancing the mind's ability to free-associate. It contains a data base of 387 broad topical categories, 61,000 idea words and phrases, and over 700,000 direct idea cross-references. It is organized around a subject-matter hierarchy with general topics at the top such as "actions-motions" and more specific subcategories at the bottom, such as "bend-flex-fold." Users can compare two sets of information at the same time and use the result to stimulate ideas. There also is a "QBank" containing questions to increase problem understanding and an IdeaPad to record all ideas. Available for both Macintosh and PC computers.

Fisher Idea Systems
2222 Martin, #110
Irvine, CA 92715
714-474-8111
Price: $95

Idea Generator Plus

This program guides the user through a three-step problem-solving process: (1) Describe the situation, (2) Generate ideas, and (3) Evaluate the ideas. The idea generation stage relies on such techniques as metaphors, analogies, and thinking about how someone else might solve the problem. It is available for DOS-based computers.

Experience in Software
2000 Hearst Avenue
Berkeley, CA 94709
800-678-7008
Price: $195

IdeGen++

IdeGen++ contains five modules: (1) Ideas, (2) Evaluate, (3) Sort, (4) Print, and (5) Idea Pad. One distinctive feature of the Ideas phase is the use of "distant models" which are similar to the Tickler boosters in this book. Distant models consist of a variety of unrelated stimulus words that are used to prompt creative ideas. Available for both Macintosh and PC computers.

FinnTrade, Inc.
5874 Doyle Street, Suite 11
Emeryville, CA 94608
415-547-2281
Price: $495

MindLink Problem Solver

This program is based on the "Synectics" approach to creative problem solving, which relies on analogies to disrupt conventional thinking and spark ideas. Users are guided through different problem-solving activities using a "HyperCard" interface. "Triggers" (unrelated stimulus words and phrases) are used to stimulate ideas. The program also contains an "idea gym" that helps loosen up the mind. Available for both Macintosh and PC computers.

MindLink, Inc.
Box 247
North Pomfret, VT 05053
802-457-2025
Price: $299

The Solution Machine

The Solution is similar to the MindLink Problem Solver in that it also is based on the Synectics approach. However, it uses a different problem solving approach involving seven stages: (1) Describe the problem freely—generate definitions, (2) Describe the problem in an action statement, (3) Rate the problem for difficulty, (4) Introduce and develop an imaginary situation, (5) Generate ideas using "connect-a-phors"—specific metaphors to suggest ideas, (6) Refine the "Connect-a-phors," and (7) Evaluate the ideas using the plus/minus inventory. Available for both Macintosh and PC computers.

The Gemini Group
R.D. 2, Box 117
Bedford, NY 10506
914-764-4938
Price: $149

References

Andersen, H.R. *The Idea of the Diamond Idea Group.* Chicago: Mitsubishi Heavy Industries America, 1991.

Buzan, T. *Use Both Sides of Your Brain.* New York: Dutton, 1976.

Clark, C.H. *The Crawford Slip Writing Method.* Kent, OH: Charles H. Clark, 1978.

Crawford, C.C., & Demidovitch, J.W. *Crawford Slip Writing Method: How to Mobilize Brainpower by Think Tank Tehnology.* Los Angeles, CA: University of Southern California, School of Public Administration, 1983.

Crovitz, H.F. *Galton's Walk.* New York: Harper & Row, 1970.

De Bono, E. *Lateral Thinking for Management.* New York: American Management Association, 1972.

Delbecq, A.L., & Van de Ven, A.H. "A Group Process Model for Problem Identification and Program Planning." *Journal of Applied Behavioral Science* 7 (1971): 466-492.

Faafeng, O. Conversation with author. Oslo: Norwegian Management Institute, 1986.

Geschka, H. "Methods and Organization of Idea Management." Paper presented at Creativity Development Week II, Greensboro, NC: Center for Creative Leadership, 1979.

Geschka, H., Schaude, G.R., & Schlicksupp, H. "Modern Techniques for Solving Problems." *Chemical Engineering* (August, 1973): 91-97.

Geschka, H., von Reibnitz, U., & Storvik, K. *Idea Generation Methods: Creative Solutions to Business and Technical Problems.* Columbus, OH: Battelle Memorial Institute, 1981.

Goodman, J., & Shields, J.T. *Brainwriting: Is There Life After Brainstorming?* St. Louis, MO: Maritz Performance Improvement Company, 1993.

Gordon, W.J.J. *Synectics.* New York: Harper & Row, 1961.

Griggs, R.E. "A Storm of Ideas." *Training* 22 (1985): 66.

Grossman, S. "Releasing Problem Solving Energies." *Training and Development Journal* 38 (1984): 94-98.

Grossman, S., & Catlin, K. "SuperHeroes." Paper presented at the 31st Annual Creative Problem Solving Institute. Buffalo, NY: The Creative Education Foundation, 1985.

Haefele, J. *Creativity and Innovation.* New York: Van Nostrand Reinhold, 1961.

Hall, D. *Jump Start Your Brain.* New York: Time-Warner, 1994.

Hammer, M., & Champy, J. *Reengineering the Corporation.* New York: HarperBusiness, 1993.

Kepner, C.H., & Tregoe, B.B. *The New Rational Manager.* Princeton, NJ: Kepner-Tregoe, 1981.

Koberg, D., & Bagnall, J. *The Universal Traveler.* Los Altos, CA: William Kaufmann, 1976.

MacCrimmon, K.R., & Taylor, R.N. "Decision Making and Problem Solving." In *Handbook of Industrial and Organizational Psychology* edited by M.D. Dunnette. Chicago: Rand McNally, 1976.

Michalko, M. *ThinkerToys.* Berkeley, CA: Ten Speed Press, 1991.

Olson, R.W. *The Art of Creative Thinking.* New York: Barnes & Noble, 1980.

Osborn, A.F. *Applied Imagination,* 3d ed. New York: Scribner and Sons, 1963.

Pearson, A.W. "Communication, Creativity, and Commitment: A Look at the Collective Notebook Approach." In *Proceedings of Creativity Week* I, edited by S.S. Gruskiewicz. Greensboro, NC: Center for Creative Leadership, 1978.

Phillips, D.J. "Report on Discussion 66." *Adult Education Journal* 7 (1948): 181-182.

Pickens, J. *Brainsketching.* Norman, OK: University of Oklahoma, 1980.

Pickens, J. Conversation with author, 1985.

"Plugging in to Creativity." *U.S. News & World Report* (October 29, 1990).

Rickards, T. *Problem Solving Through Creative Analysis.* Essex, UK: Gower Press, 1974.

Schaude, G.R. "Methods of Idea Generation." Paper presented at Creativity Development Week I, Greensboro, NC: Center for Creative Leadership, 1978.

Simon, H.A. *The New Science of Management Decision,* rev. ed. Englewood Cliffs, NJ: Prentice-Hall, 1977.

Souder, W.E., & Ziegler, R.W. "A Review of Creativity and Problem Solving Techniques." *Research Management* (July, 1977): 34-42.

Tauber, E.M. "HIT: Heuristic Ideation Technique—A Systematic Procedure for New Product Search." *Journal of Marketing* 36 (1972): 58-61.

Taylor, J.W. *How To Create Ideas.* Englewood Cliffs, NJ: Prentice-Hall, 1961.

VanGundy, A.B. *Circles of Creativity.* Norman, OK: VanGundy & Associates, 1985.

VanGundy, A.B. *Idea Power: Techniques and Resources to Unleash the Creativity in Your Organization.* New York: AMACOM, 1992.

VanGundy, A.B. *Managing Group Creativity: A Modular Approach to Problem Solving.* New York: AMACOM, 1984.

VanGundy, A.B. *Overcoming Productivity Losses in Brainstorming and Brainwriting Groups.* Norman, OK: Communication Department, University of Oklahoma, forthcoming.

VanGundy, A.B. *Techniques of Structured Problem Solving,* 2d ed. New York: Van Nostrand Reinhold, 1988.

VanGundy, A.B. *108 Ways to Get a Bright Idea.* Englewood Cliffs, NJ: Prentice-Hall, 1983.

Wakin, E. "Component Detailing." Paper presented at the 31st Annual Creative Problem Solving Institute. Buffalo, NY: Creative Education Foundation, 1985.

Warfield, J.N., Geschka, H., & Hamilton, R. *Methods of Idea Management.* Columbus, OH: The Academy for Contemporary Problems, 1975.

Whiting, C.S. *Creative Thinking.* New York: Van Nostrand Reinhold, 1958.

Woods, M.F. "The Brainwriting Game." *Creativity Network* 5 (1979): 7-12.

Wycoff, J. *Mindmapping: Your Personal Guide to Exploring Creativity and Problem-Solving.* New York: Berkley Books, 1991.

Zwicky, F. *Discovery, Invention, Research Through the Morphological Approach.* New York: Macmillan, 1969.

Index

noun-modifier, 139-140
from problem attributes,
144-146
using action verbs,
176-178
Frito-Lay, 7
Fry, Art, 29
Fun.
See also Humor; Playfulness
for groups, 42
during idea generation,
303-305
"Fuzzy" problems, 12

G

Gallery Method, 292
Gender differences, in
problem solving, 260-262
Geschka, Horst, 285, 287,
292
"Get Crazy" booster, 70-72
"Get Real!!" booster,
234-235
Gordon, William, 167, 255
Gordon/Little Method, 167,
255
"Grab Bag Forced
Association" booster, 270
"Grab bag" method, 41, 59,
197-219
Graphics
for idea prompting, 298
for representing
problems, 132-134
"Greeting Cards" booster,
311-312
Grossman, Steve, 203
Group brain boosters, 39-
40, 42-47, 222-322.
See also Brain boosters;
Individual brain boosters
brainstorming with
related boosters, 225-257
brainstorming with un-
related boosters, 259-282

brainwriting with related
boosters, 283-298
brainwriting with
unrelated boosters,
299-322
organization of, 46-47
"top ten," 49
Group climate, healthy, 226
"Group Not" booster,
288-290
Groups
enhancing creativity in,
253-254
increasing participation
in, 241-242
motivating, 268-269
playful atmosphere in,
310-312
points for working with,
42-43
problem clarification in,
245-249
Guidance, from an "inner
voice," 178-179

H

Habit-bound thinking, 26-27
Haefele, John, 293
Hall, Doug, 33, 134, 151,
186, 189, 199, 228, 239,
243, 250, 262
Hammer, Michael, 7
Hands-on brain booster
tools, 324-325
Heimel, Cynthia, 17
Heuristic Ideation Technique
(HIT), 141
Home computers, improve-
ment of, 248-249
"Home run" ideas, 9
Human resource problems,
brain boosters for, 55-56
Humor.
See also Fun; Playfulness
encouraging, 42
link to creativity, 311

I

BRAIN BOOSTERS FOR BUSINESS ADVANTAGE

Visual thinking, 270

W

"Wake Up Call" booster,
83-85
Warfield, John, 285
"We Have Met the Problem
and It Is Us" booster,
191-193
*Whack on the Side of the
Head*, A (van Oech), 324
"What can be," exploring,
166
"What If...?" booster,
193-195
"What if" method, 41
"What Is It?" booster,
218-220
"What's the Problem?"
booster, 254-257
"Wild and crazy" ideas, 227
Word combinations, idea
stimulation via, 122-124
"Word Diamond" booster,
152-155
Words
combining in problem
statements, 153-155
as idea prompters,
116-118, 178
use in idea generation,
138
Writing, creative, 97-101
Wycoff, Joyce, 160

Y

"You're a Card, Andy!"
booster, 296-297
"Your Slip Is Showing"
booster, 297-298

- **Cover Concept**

  Tom Lewis, Inc.

- **Cover Design Execution,
  Project Coordinator, and
  Interior Text Design**

  Susan G. Odelson

- **Illustrations**

  Lee Ann Hubbard

- **Editorial Staff**

  Heidi Erika Callinan,
  JoAnn Padgett,
  Susan Rachmeler, and
  Katharine Pechtimaldjian